MINI COOPER

& COOPER'S

Graham Robson

CONTENTS

Foulis

Haynes

ISBN 0 85429 445 7

A FOULIS Motorcycling Book

First published 1984

© **Haynes Publishing Group**

Published by:
Haynes Publishing Group
Sparkford, Yeovil,
Somerset BA22 7JJ

Haynes Publications Inc.
861 Lawrence Drive, Newbury
Park, California 91320 USA

**British Library Cataloguing in
Publication Data**
Robson, Graham
    Mini Cooper super profile
    1. Morris Mini Minor automobile
    I. Title
    629.2'222   TL215.M615
    ISBN 0–85429–445–7

Editor: Rod Grainger
Dust jacket design: Rowland Smith
Page Layout: Mike King
Colour photographs: By Andrew
Morland, taken especially for
this book and from the
J. Baker Collection
Road tests: Courtesy of *Motor*
Printed in England by: J.H. Haynes &
Co. Ltd

FOREWORD

Everyone, I am sure, admired the Mini-Cooper, even those people regularly beaten up by them in traffic, out-manoeuvred on the road, or ousted from the winner's circle in rallying, autocross, or on the race track. All Coopers — big-engined or small-engined, race-tuned or standard — were so remarkable that you had to be impressed. I know I always was.

If it was Sir Alec Issigonis who invented the Mini itself, it was John Cooper, of Grand Prix racing fame, who first thought of the Mini-Cooper. Issigonis provided the front-wheel-drive, the peerless handling, and the remarkable packaging, but it was John Cooper's enthusiasm which helped provide the extra performance the little car so richly deserved.

It proved to be a far more versatile, and attractive, concept than BMC's directors could ever have hoped. In 1961, when the original long-stroke derivative was launched, it was looked upon as a rather nice, but probably short-lived marketing indulgence — but by 1971, when the last cars were being built here in the UK, it had turned into a truly profitable project.

Even though Lord Stoke's British Leyland combine killed off the whole Mini-Cooper concept, we must never forget that it lived on, mechanically if not in name, in the Italian-built Innocentis for several more years.

Factually, I am sure, almost everything is already known about the life and times of the Mini-Coopers, and the Mini-Cooper S cars which stemmed from them, for there are racing classes, and thriving specialist Companies, which concentrate on them to this day. I hope, however, that this *Super Profile* not only adds its tribute to a great series of cars, but provides just that important little extra background about them.

The first Mini-Cooper I ever saw was competing in a British rally, and I am quite sure I need not stress that it was beating the pants off every other car in sight. That was in 1961. In the decade which followed, I observed 'works' cars winning the Monte Carlo Rally several times (and being robbed, once) and the 'works Cooper Cars' examples performing miracles on the race track: I even found time to sit alongside virtuoso Cooper drivers in some of those events and to admire their skills as well as the competence of the car. Even so, I have to say that there was always, a limit to what the Mini Coopers could achieve. Their wheels were too small, their transmission weak, their suspension too hard, and their understeer untameable. Their drivers — on road or track — were more than happy to put up with these foibles, so Coopers sold, and sold, and sold ... Looking at modern sports saloons — VW Golf GTI, Escort XR3i, or whatever — it seems that all were inspired by the Mini-Cooper.

I, too, was inspired by the Mini Cooper but I could not have compiled this little book without a lot of help, and I would like to thank several people for this:

The factual research into Mini-Cooper production could not be done without help from Anders Clausager, of BL Heritage, at Studley.

Ray Holman, David Nutland, Keith Redwood and Stephen Scadding of the Mini-Cooper Club very kindly found cars for photography.

Andrew Morland and Mirco Decet also helped enormously, where illustration was concerned.

Stuart Turner, now an important power in the land at Ford, provided much background information about the birth, and the development of the Mini-Cooper S.

Lastly, of course, my grateful thanks to Sir Alec Issigonis, and to John Cooper, for creating these delightful little cars in the first place.

Graham Robson

HISTORY

In their day the Mini-Coopers were astonishing little cars. It wasn't just that they were so agile, so fast for their size, or so successful in motorsport — it was the fact that they were being built at all, and by BMC of all people! But the BMC of the mid-1960s was radically different from that of the 1950s, which was a great relief to every motoring enthusiast.

BMC had been formed in 1952, by the fusion of Austin with the Nuffield Organisation, and it was soon apparent that Austin, and its chairman, Leonard Lord, was going to rule the roost. The next few years saw many interesting, individual and well-known models disappear, to be replaced by families of cars, engines and transmissions, mostly inspired by Longbridge.

After the world of motoring had been shocked out of its postwar complacency by the first great Suez crisis, Alec Issigonis's little team designed the revolutionary AD015 (Austin Drawing Office number) Mini, complete wiith transverse engine, transmission in the sump, and front-wheel-drive — persuaded BMC's directors to back it, and saw it put on sale in the autumn of 1959. Then, there were two distinct 'names' for the same product — the Austin Seven, and the Morris Mini-Minor. It wasn't long, however, before we motorists christened them all 'Minis', and the name eventually stuck.

The original Mini was almost laughably under-developed, as book after book has shown. What with the legendary floating carpets (due to water leaks through the floor), engines with ignition systems that went on strike in heavy rain, and the music hall jokes about big dogs cocking legs against the open (sliding!) windows, it was a miracle that the Mini survived.

But it did — not least because of its amazing packaging (as John Cooper once said: 'As small as a telephone box outside, as big as the Albert Hall inside') was backed by extremely compact dimensions, and its front-wheel-drive handling and steering was a real joy. By comparison with any other BMC saloon car of the day, it was a miracle — it was a truly nimble little ten foot long box which cried out for more power.

BMC, or more particularly Alec Issigonis's design team, were in no hurry to provide faster Minis. For one reason, Issigonis was completely wedded to the idea of the Mini being a tiny economy car, and for another, his engineers were already fully-committed to the development of the next range of front-wheel-drive cars, the 1100s.

At this point, however, John Cooper, whose Grand Prix cars had already won the World Championship, and whose Formula Junior cars used racetuned BMC A-series engines (basically the same type of engine as the Mini's), comes into the story. At an early stage he had borrowed a Mini, driven it to Italy, and been depressed by its lack of speed and acceleration. But he had also lent it to Ferrari's team manager for a trial — he came back, handed the keys to Cooper and commented: 'If it wasn't so ugly, I would shoot myself!'

Cooper had already wasted months trying to make a Renault Dauphine handle properly when equipped with a Coventry-Climax engine — and failed. Now he determined to make a *real* little sports saloon out of the Mini. The original 'hot' Mini had probably been built by Daniel Richmond, at Downton Engineering, but what we might call the prototype Mini-Cooper was built by John Cooper's business in Surbiton. Cooper then tried to 'sell' the idea to Alec Issigonis, could not divert him from his crusade to provide ultra-safe economy motoring for the millions, and had to appeal direct to BMC's managing director, George Harriman, to approve a sanction of 1000 cars to be built at Longbridge.

The 1000 was necessary to secure sporting homologation into Group 2, for John Cooper was determined to see the Mini winning on the race tracks; Cooper's 'fee' for this quick development and 'selling' job was that his name appeared on every car, and under the agreement he had with Harriman, a small royalty was paid to him for every car built. The latter was no more than a nice gesture from BMC when 1000 cars were in prospect — but after ten years, and getting on for 150,000 Mini-Coopers of all types Cooper's finances had benefited considerably!

Two years after the original BMC Mini had been announced, the Mini-Cooper was launched. Visually it was almost identical with the standard Minis except for the different grilles and badging: even inside the car the only noticeable changes were to the simple facia panel, and the provision of a remote control gearchange. There were no body sheet metal changes, no wider-rim wheels, no suspension changes, no transmission changes — nothing.

The secrets of the Mini-Cooper's performance advances were in the engine, and the braking system. To stop the little car, which would have a top speed approaching 90mph, compared with the 72mph normally achieved by the 850cc Mini, BMC persuaded Lockheed to produce their smallest-ever disc caliper design for the front brakes, though the 850's standard rear drums were retained, and there was no need for a servo booster.

The A-series engine, of course, had already been around for ten years. It had started as an 803cc engine for the A30 and Morris Minor, been enlarged to 948cc for the A35/Minor 1000/Austin-Healey Sprite, reduced to 848cc for the front-drive Minis, then was in the process of being pushed out to 1,098cc for the next generation of BMC front-wheel-drive saloons, the AD016 1100s, so the choice of engine capacity for the Mini-Cooper was wide enough already.

To get it cosily up to the 1-litre sporting capacity limit, however, BMC decided not to use their existing 948cc engine size which had been used in original Mini prototypes of 1958, and the contemporary Sprite/Midget sports cars, but to create a new size altogether. The original Cooper, therefore, was given a 997cc engine, having a bore of 62.43mm and a stroke of 81.28mm (2.46 x 3.20in in good old 'British' measure!): at the time it was stated that this new capacity was' related to a degree of rationalisation of engine strokes which is planned for future power units ...'

In fact this reasoning was flawed, reflecting rather confused thinking (nothing unusual in that, at BMC, in the 1960s!), for these bore and stroke dimensions resulted in a rather old-fashioned long-stroke configuration not ideal for super-tuning, and the 'degree of rationalisation' did not happen until 1964, when the 1275S appeared and the 997cc Cooper had already gone. No other BMC A-series engine ever used the 81.28mm stroke ... Nowadays it seems to be agreed that BMC should have gone for the 998cc 'enlarged 948cc' solution at once – but it took more than two years for them to decide to do so.

Just to line up the various A-series derivatives of the period:

	Bore and stroke (mm)
850 Mini (848cc)	62.9 x 68.3
A35/Minor 1000/Spridget (948cc)	62.9 x 76.2
997 Mini-Cooper (997cc)	62.43 x 81.28
Future 1100 unit (1098cc)	64.58 x 83.72
Riley Elf/Hornet/998 Cooper (998cc)	64.58 x 76.2

– and there was more to come!

To complement the enlarged engine size of the 997cc Mini-Cooper, there was also a different camshaft profile, a higher compression ratio, twin semi-downdraught 1 1/4in. SU carbs instead of a single instrument, and a fabricated exhaust system. The result was a very creditable power boost, from 34bhp at 5500rpm for the 850 Mini, to 55bhp at 6000 for the Mini Cooper – a 62 per cent improvement, from an 18 per cent capacity change!

Even in its original, and standard, form, the Mini-Cooper was an impressive little car, though at a quarter of a century's range it no longer seems to be all that quick. A top speed of 85mph, and 0-60mph time of 18 seconds can, after all, now be beaten by just about every Mini Metro on the market ... But in 1961, when it was announced, that performance made the Cooper quicker than the then current MG Midget in all respects, so no-one was complaining.

There were also the facts that the engine proved itself to be tuneable, long stroke or not, that the roadholding and agility, even on cross-ply tyres and 3.5in rims, was peerless, and that there was a thriving Mini 'accessory' industry ready to provide everything from a locking filler cap to a steering column rake adjuster, a wood-rimmed steering wheel to an oil cooler, a special seat to an engine tune-up kit. To run an unmodified Mini-Cooper somehow seemed to brand one as a wimp, or a Wally (though we hadn't invented either name in those innocent days ...) Already the 850 Mini was a successful competition car in its class, and the Mini-Cooper

improved dramatically on that. When Pat Moss won the 1962 Tulip rally outright (on handicap, I must admit), it had truly made its mark.

To keep the story neat and tidy, I ought to mention the Mini-Cooper change from 997cc and 998cc at this point. It was not quite as simple as it sounds, for that 1cc difference was actually achieved by abandoning the original, special, Mini-Cooper bore/ stroke dimensions, and by substituting the later Riley Elf/Wolseley Hornet 'Mini' engine, with a new head casting in Cooper tune, in its place. The Elf/Hornet engine was really an amalgam of the 948/1100 block and 64.58mm cylinder bore, with the original A30/A35/Sprite stroke of 76.2mm (or exactly 3.0 inches, in Imperial measure).

The peak power output of 55bhp, as claimed by BMC, was not changed, though the torque figure was slightly enhanced. The effect on the car's performance though not dramatic, was significant: test cars with the 998cc engine could reach 90mph (a 5mph improvement), and reach 60mph in about 16.5 seconds (a 1.5 second improvement), which suggests to me that there had been a power increase after all, or that BMC's original claim for the long-stroke 997cc Mini-Cooper had been a shade optimistic.

There was another minor, but significant change soon afterwards, when radial ply tyres were standardised, but the major change followed in the autumn of 1964, when the original rubber cone type of front suspension was replaced by Hydrolastic suspension, which had been introduced for the Morris 1100 car of 1962. The suspension's basic layout was not changed, but it now seemed to be somewhat softer. The unique rubber/liquid chamber interface, and the narrow pipe interconnection from front to rear Hydrolastic units, rather destroyed the original cars' marvellous stability in the interests of a softer ride. The theory was that as the front wheels rose to climb over a road hump, they signalled to the rear suspension to raise the body accordingly – but, in practice, the overall effect was never quite right. Hydrolastic suspension, in fact, was not a great success on Minis, a model for which it was abandoned in 1969, though it lived on in the Mini-Cooper S (and the 1100/1300 models) to the bitter end.

The important advance, however, had come in March 1963, with the launch of the original Mini-Cooper S, actually with a 1071cc engine. Once again the chassis required very little attention, for the only changes were to specify radial ply tyres, larger front disc brakes, a brake vacuum servo, and offer wheels with 4.5in rim width as options. The big improvement, more fundamental than BMC admitted at the time, was to the engine.

John Cooper had seen that Mini-Coopers could not win many races, and therefore championships, with a long-stroke 1-litre engine, and at the same time he saw the limitations the same type of engine imposed on his single-seater Formula Junior cars. In conjunction with BMC, therefore,

and especially the resourceful Eddie Maher (a senior development engineer at the Morris Engines branch, whose roots could be traced back to the high performance Riley engines of the 1930s), Cooper inspired the development of a much modified power unit which looked very much as before, to a casual glance, but was very different indeed in detail.

In its existing form, the A-series engine had already run out of development 'stretch', for with the 64.58mm cylinder bores planned for the new 1100s there was very little metal indeed left between the bores, and the bore/stroke ratio was still very undersquare. The new 'Formula Junior' cylinder block developed for Cooper, however, not only featured larger big-end journals (2.0 in diameter instead of 1.75in, making them as large as the mains) and a nitrided crankshaft, but had a cylinder block with different bore spacing.

To allow for larger cylinder bores, but without changing the external profile of the block, the cylinder centre positions were changed. The distance between the middle pair of cylinders was decreased by 0.25in, while that between cylinders 1 and 2, and 3 and 4, was increased by 0.25in; the

whole chain of barrels was 'siamesed', which is to say that no cooling water could circulate right around them. Strictly speaking, this was 'illegal' in Formula Junior terms, for it meant that a standard cylinder block casting was no longer being used – but the fact was that for 1961 the Cooper-BMC 'works' cars run by Ken Tyrrell were able to use 1.1-litres, and more power! Competition customers were offered similar units for 1962.

This development, please note, was a full two years ahead of the launch of the Mini-Cooper S, and several months ahead of the launch of the original 997cc Mini-Cooper. Stuart Turner, who became BMC's competitions manager in the autumn of 1961, has recently confirmed that the Mini-Cooper S engine programme (and development of the car itself) was already under way when he arrived at Abingdon.

Right from the start, it seems, BMC and John Cooper were looking for engines enlarged to the 1.3-litre sporting class limit, and also producing a high-revving, ultra-strong, little short-stroke 1-litre unit. In both of these cases, however, new and unique crankshaft machining would be needed, and the original 'interim'

Mini-Cooper engine dimensions

Engine size	Bore and stroke (mm)	Model used	Comment
848	62.9 x 68.26	850 Mini from 1959	Short-stroke version of 948cc engine
948	62.9 x 76.2	'Standard' engine from 1956	As used on many BMC cars
997	62.43 x 81.28	997 Mini-Cooper from 1961	Reduced bore, long stroke unique then, but to be used on 1275S
998	64.58 x 76.2	998 Mini-Cooper from 1964	'Standard' 948cc/1098cc block with enlarged bore from 1098cc unit, and stroke from 948cc unit!
970S	70.6 x 61.91	970 Mini-Cooper S from 1964	New 'S'-type block, with unique short stroke
1071S	70.6 x 68.26	1071 Mini-Cooper S from 1963	New 'S'-type block, allied to 848cc stroke!
1275S	70.6 x 81.28	1275 Mini-Cooper S from 1964	New 'S'-type block, allied to original 997 Mini-Cooper stroke.

– and, to add to the confusion ...

994	64.2 x 76.2	Original Cooper-BMC Formula Junior engine	Enlarged bore version of 'standard' 948cc block.
1095	67.6 x 76.2	Enlarged Cooper-BMC Formula Junior engine, first raced in 1961	Special cylinder block, effectively Mini-Cooper S prototypes, but with standard 76.2 strokes, and slightly reduced cylinder bore to suit.

1071S only came about as a stop-gap measure, because it used the new large-bore cylinder block with the crankshaft throws, and therefore the stroke, of the existing 848cc Mini.

This could be confusing, so please see the adjacent table of all the various engine dimensions used by Mini-Coopers between 1961 and 1971.

The definitive Mini-Cooper S, of course, not only in terms of performance, but in terms of the quantities manufactured, and the length of time it was on sale, was the 76bhp 1275S, and compared with this car, the other two S-types are only side shows. According to the production figures provided by BL (which cannot, in fact, be authenticated in detail) no fewer than 40,449 1275S models were built, which compares with a mere 972 970S models, and 4017 1071S models.

BMC however, needed to make no excuses for this. The 1071S, in their eyes, was definitely only an interim model, which went out of production as soon as supplies of the 970S and 1275S versions began to build up (it had a life, in fact, of just 16 months), while the 970S was an acknowledged, but very honestly marketed, 'homologation special'.

With the release of the 1275S in March 1964 (and volume production getting under way in April), the Cooper S programme reached maturity. Even before this time, the Mini-Coopers had proved to be excellent competition cars, but from now on they were to be truly formidable.

EVOLUTION

The 'S' Story

Even though BMC, and John Cooper, always looked on the Mini-Cooper S as a basic competition car, there were still many compromises in the standard specification. For years, for instance, it was a standing joke that the engine tune was suppressed by a very mild camshaft profile, so that 'the district nurse could use it for house calls'; that there were complaints about the lack of instruments (no rev counter was ever fitted to a Mini-Cooper, for instance); and constant complaints about the amount of work, and the buying of extras, needed to produce a full-blooded competition car.

It meant, however, that parts business was brisk, and that the list of options grew and grew. The wide-rim wheels essential for racing or rallying were never standardised (though BMC would certainly fit them, at extra cost, when the car was being manufactured), while twin fuel tanks and an engine cooler, previously optional, were only standardised at the end of 1965 when they were needed for Group 1 sporting homologation in 1966!

Having bought the car, however, you could immediately start to buy high-performance items such as stronger, straight-cut gears, modified suspension units, engine tune up kits, wheel arch extension kits and ... need I go on? And these were just a few of the options from the factory. Accessory firms chimed in with special seats, steering wheels, steering column adjusters, dampers, instrumentation packs, wind-up window conversions, 'nerfing bars' (extra large bumpers), switchgear, and countless other parts.

For an 'off-the-line' car, however, you started in 1963 by buying the 1071S, volume production of which began in April 1963, and ran out at the end of August 1964. As with all pre-1970 model Mini-Coopers, there were Austins and Morrises, but both were built on the same assembly lines at Longbridge (really, the old 'Austin' factory), with chassis numbers all in the mass of Mini derivatives — saloons, estate cars, vans and pickups — being made at that time. No Mini-Cooper of any type was ever built at Cowley, or anywhere else in the UK.

The 970S and 1275S models were revealed in March 1964, when BMC emphasised that all three S-types — 970, 1071 and 1275cc — would continue to be available in the future. Visually there was no way of identifying a car from outside, and even under the bonnet it needed an expert, and practised, eye to pick out the slightly deeper cylinder block of the long-stroke 1275S. The 970S, of course gave itself away on the road by being the more obviously high-revving machine, while the 1275S had a more boomy and deep throated exhaust note and a distinct engine roughness in the early models.

Although both new S-Types were announced together, series production had not yet begun. The first track-built 1275S took shape on February 10, 1964, and volume production followed in April, but the very first track-built 970S did not follow until June 1964. The 970S then remained in steady production, at a rate of about 20 cars a week, until withdrawn in April 1965.

It was a truly frenetic year for changes to Mini-Coopers. The first 998cc cars had been built on November 20, 1963 (and the last 997cc car on December 4 — there being a slight overlap), but public announcement had followed in January 1964. Next came the launch of the 970S and 1275S, after which (unannounced, but widely expected) the 1071S was finally dropped on August 28.

This meant that Hydrolastic suspension, fitted progressively to all other Mini saloons from September/October 1964, was never applied to the 1071S, but it found its place in the 998cc Mini-Cooper, the 970S and the 1275S as well. Incidentally, even though Hydrolastic was dropped from the ordinary Minis when Austin and Morris badges were dropped in 1969 (and when the winding window specification was standardised), it was never dropped from the specification of the 1275S.

The 970S had a short, but busy, 11 month life. A study of the Longbridge Mini 'chassis books' shows that two blocks of numbers, 1000 each for the Austin and Morris versions (making 2000 in all) were originally reserved, but that only a total of 972 cars were actually built. To be precise, there were 262 'dry' Austins and 292 'dry' Morris versions, with 230 'wet' Austins and 188 'wet' Morris types.

Thereafter, Longbridge concentrated on building more (and more, and more ...) 1275S derivatives, which sold all round the world, and which seemed to be suitable for *any* type of motorsport. From 1964 to 1971 1275S cars remained basically the same, though there were many development changes, major and minor. Apart from the announcement of the MkII model for 1968, and the 'unbadged' MkIII of March 1970, there was also the rather indeterminate introduction of an all-synchromesh gearbox during 1968 (it was indeterminate because it was not a clean and positive introduction – British Leyland, especially the old BMC sector, was like that, at the time), and the standardisation of the twin fuel tanks and an oil cooler from the beginning of 1966.

All, however, is not as simple as it seems, for many 1275Ss were built with the oil cooler and twin tanks (*and* wide-rim wheels) during 1965 when they were still optional extras! Other important development changes included the provision of a diaphragm spring clutch from September 1964, a reclining front seat option from the end of 1965, and higher-rated Hydrolastic units, plus solid (rather than rubber) inboard driveshaft universal joints from the spring of 1966.

Although the MkIII car, announced in March 1970, was much improved in some ways (such as the concealed-hinge body shell with wind-up windows, and Mini-Clubman trim and seating), it would also be true to say that British Leyland had only reluctantly put that car on sale at all. One important policy decision, made soon after the new corporation was founded, was to let 'Mini' become a marque in its own right, by deleting the Austin and Morris badges, just as the buying public had been doing for years. Another, taken so it is said, by Lord Stokes and his top advisers, was to get rid of all consultancy and royalty agreements as rapidly as possible. The result was that Daniel Richmond's invaluable Downton Engineering link was cast aside, and the names of 'Healey' and 'Cooper' were dropped, Healey at the end of 1970. The last Mini-Cooper S produced in the UK, was built in July 1971.

From the autumn of 1966, the 1275cc engine, in de-tuned form, was fitted to the Austin-Healey Sprite/MG Midget models, and from the summer of 1967 it also became available in the BMC '1100' saloons as well. Even in the Sprite/Midget, when rated at 65bhp, it was different in many ways, not only in terms of valve sizes, but in terms of camshaft profiles, and a different head casting too! Complicated!

There was some overseas assembly of Mini-Coopers (mainly 998cc and 1275cc S), mainly from CKD Kits, in fact S-types continued to be built in Australia for some time after Longbridge had wound up the project, and there was also the very successful production of Innocenti Minis, by De Tomaso in Italy.

The Innocenti products were not 'pure' Mini-Cooper S, in that there were styling changes even to the basic model, and in that the definitive Innocenti Mini had an entirely different squared-up body style, shaped by Bertone, and complete with a hatchback. It is notoriously difficult to get any sort of reliable production figures from Italian concerns these days, so I can only say, with confidence, that there was effectively a Bertone-bodied Mini-Cooper S, badged as an Innocenti, in production in Milan until 1982, rated at 71bhp (DIN), just about the same as the 76bhp Mini-Cooper S would have been if measured by the more strict DIN systems.

Little needs to be said, here, about the Mini-Cooper's success in motorsport, for its private-owner career is still continuing, and its 'works' record has been chronicled very accurately by Peter Browning in another Haynes publication, *The Works Minis*. It is enough for me to point out that the 997cc Mini-Cooper was announced in the autumn of 1961, and won the Tulip Rally (Pat Moss driving) on only its second outing, that the 1071S was announced in March 1963 and won the Touring category of the Alpine Rally in June 1963, and that the 1275S was announced in March 1964 and won the Tulip rally outright just a month later!

Cars prepared by the Cooper Car Co. were victorious in the European Touring Car Championship, and here in the UK (where they were sometimes beaten by cars prepared by Ralph Broad's Broadspeed organisation!), while works and private cars soon took a hold on the TV-inspired rallycross scene. In autotests they were supreme, in hillclimbing they could be competitive; on any doubtful surface, where their front-wheel-drive grip and agility helped, they could be unbeatable.

Old age caught up with the Mini-Cooper S in rallying when it began to explore the outer limits of front-wheel-drive technology, and when real homologation specials like the Ford Escort Twin-Cam arrived. Properly marketed, however, the Mini-Cooper S was still a successful road car into the early 1970s, suffering only in the same way as *all* Minis were suffering, by looking the same as ever, and not being any faster or more reliable, and little better equipped than they had been for several years past.

By 1971, the Austin-Morris division of British Leyland was lurching towards financial trouble, and George Turnbull's management team looked around for ways to economise. In a general programme of retrenchment, it was decided to cut back on what I call 'fringe' Mini products. The 998cc Mini-Cooper, the Riley Elf and the Wolseley Hornet all disappeared in 1969, and after a short life in MkIII form, so did the 1275S. The long-nosed Mini Clubman had arrived in 1969, and with it the 1275GT, but this was but a pale shadow of the 1275S it was supposed to supersede, and few people had a good word to say for it. It deserves no more than a passing mention in this book.

Now, in the 1980s, there are several cars with a flavour of Mini-Cooper S in their make-up – MG Metro Turbo, Ford Escort XR3i, and Golf GTi to name but a few. The Mini-Cooper needs no better epitaph than that.

Evolution summary — all Cooper models

Although the basic layout and design of Mini-Coopers never changed, in the ten years that they were on the market, there were many significant development changes, or additional models, in that period.

September 1961. The original Mini-Coopers, badged as Austins or Morrises, were introduced, with long-stroke 997cc engines, and tiny front disc-brakes. The 'Cooper' name came from that of the Cooper Car Co., famous racing car manufacturers. The engine, incidentally, was a BMC A-series derivative, but the capacity was never used in any other BMC car.

March 1963. The original Mini-Cooper S, the 1071S, was introduced, also with Austin and Morris badging. The engine was a big-bore/short-stroke development of the original, with revised cylinder bore centres, more robust bottom end, and more potential.

January 1964. The 997cc Mini-Cooper engine gave way to the 998cc version, this engine having a bigger bore/shorter stroke than the original, and being shared in basic form with Riley Elf/Wolseley Hornet 'Minis'. A change to help rationalisation, rather than performance.

March 1964. The original 1071S was joined by two further Mini-Cooper S models, the 65bhp short-stroke 970S, and the 76bhp long-stroke 1275S — the smaller car being an 'homologation special' specifically intended for 1-litre saloon car racing. The 1071S continued to be listed until 1965, but production ended in August 1964. 970S production, too, lasted only until April 1965, after which the 998cc and 1275cc cars were left in production.

September 1964. In line with all other Minis, the Mini-Cooper range was treated to Hydrolastic suspension (half rubber, half water/alcohol mixture of liquid), with front-rear 'self-correcting' interconnecting pipes.

January 1966. With an eye to Group 1 homologation (successfully achieved), the 1275S was given an upgraded specification which included twin fuel tanks, and an engine oil cooler as standard.

October 1967. In line with all Minis, the Mini-Coopers became 'MkII', with restyling touches including large rear lamps, larger back windows, and revised interior trim.

1968. In a long-drawn-out introduction, not at all clean cut, Mini-Coopers were eventually all built with the latest all-synchromesh gearbox; many 1968 models, however, still had the 'crash first gear' transmission.

October/November 1969. The 998cc Mini-Cooper was finally dropped, just before the changes listed below were phased in.

March 1970. The 1275S was given the latest AD020 type body shell, which included concealed hinges, and wind-up windows instead of sliding glass. The name was changed from Austin/Morris, to 'Mini-Cooper S'.

June 1971. UK production of Mini-Cooper S discontinued.

Note. The so-called 1275GT model, complete with long-nose body style, and single-carb 'bread-and-butter' 1275 engine, had been introduced in October 1969, and was to continue in production until August 1980. However, this car was really not at all related to the Mini-Cooper family.

SPECIFICATION

Original 997cc Mini-Cooper, produced 1961-1963

Type designation	Austin Seven Cooper/Morris Mini-Cooper
Built	Longbridge, Birmingham
Numbers manufactured	25,000 approximately (see text)
Drive configuration	Front engine, transversely mounted, front wheel drive
Engine	BMC A-Series. Four cylinders, in-line, transversely mounted across car. Cast iron cylinder block, with cast iron cylinder head. Two valves per cylinder, in line, operated by pushrods and rockers from camshaft in side (rear, in car sense) of block. Bore, stroke and capacity 62.43 x 81.28mm (2.46 x 3.20in), 997cc (60.8cu. in); 9.0:1 compression ratio. Two semi-downdraught constant-vacuum SU HS2 carburettors. Maximum power 55bhp (net) at 6000rpm. Maximum torque 54lb.ft. at 3600rpm.
Transmission	Four-speed gearbox, in unit (underneath) with transversely-mounted engine, and final drive. Four forward speeds, no synchromesh on first gear. Overall gearbox ratios: 12.05, 7.213, 5.11, 3.765; reverse 12.05:1. Helical spur gear final drive, ratio 3.765:1. (Options included close-ratio gear set, and different final drive sets).
Construction	Sheet steel unit construction two-door saloon body/chassis unit, built by BMC owned factories in Birmingham. Wheelbase 6ft 8in. (203cm) Track (front) 3ft. 11.75in. (121cm) Track (rear) 3ft. 9.9 in. (117cm)
Suspension	Front: Independent, by rubber cone springs, wishbones, and telescopic dampers. No anti-roll bar. Rear: Independent, by rubber cone springs, trailing arms, and telescopic dampers. No anti-roll bar.

Steering	Rack and pinion: 2.3 turns lock-to-lock
Brakes	Lockheed, front discs, rear drums, with no vacuum servo assistance. Front discs 7in. diameter; rear drums 7 x 1.25in. Mechanical operation of centrally-mounted handbrake.
Wheels and tyres	Pressed-steel bolt-on road wheels, with four-stud fixing. 10in. rim diameter and 3.5in. rim widths; 5.20-10in. crossply tyres. Optional 4.5in. rims.
Bodywork	All steel body style, as for all normal Minis, in two-door, four-seater layout with separate boot. Doors had sliding windows. Dimensions: overall length 10ft. 0.25in. (305cm); overall width 4ft. 7in. (139cm); overall height 4ft. 5in. (135 cm). Unladen weight (approx) 1400 lb (635 kg).
Electrical system	12 volt, 34 amp hr battery mounted in boot. Positive earth system, with Lucas components.
Fuel system	Fuel tank mounted in left side of boot, behind seats. 5.5 Imperial gallons (25 litres). Typical fuel consumption about 30mpg (9.5 litres/100km).
Performance	Source, *Autocar* 1961. Maximum speed 85mph. Maximum speeds in gears, 3rd gear 70mph; 2nd gear 46mph; 1st gear 28mph. Acceleration: 0-60mph 18.0sec; standing $\frac{1}{4}$-mile 20.9sec. Acceleration in gears: top, 20-40mph 12.5sec/50-70mph 16.7sec; third, 20-40mph 8.1sec/40-60mph 9.4sec. Fuel consumption: 23 to 34mpg (Imperial).

998cc Mini-Cooper, produced 1963-1969

Type designation	Austin Mini-Cooper/Morris Mini-Cooper
Built	Longbridge, Birmingham
Numbers manufactured	76,000 approximately (see text – total 997 and 998 production is quoted by BL as 101, 242).

Basic style, design and layout as for original 997 Mini-Cooper except for following technical differences

Engine	Bore, stroke and capacity 64.58 x 76.2mm, (2.54 x 3.00in) 998cc (60.8cu. in); 9.0:1 compression ratio. Maximum power 55bhp (net) at 5800rpm. Maximum torque 57lb.ft at 3000rpm.
Transmission	From September 1968, all-synchromesh gearbox was fitted, with overall ratios of 13.25, 8.36, 5.38, 3.765 reverse 13.328:1. No final drive change.
Suspension	From autumn 1964, Hydrolastic suspension units, with front-rear interconnection, replaced rubber cone springs, but no geometry changes.
Wheels and tyres	From March 1964, 145-10in. radial ply tyres were standardised.
Construction	As before, but MkII Model, with larger rear window, revised trim, badging, and details, introduced from October 1967.
Performance	Source *Autocar* 1965. Maximum speed 90mph. Maximum speeds in gears, 3rd gear 68mph; 2nd gear 51mph, 1st gear 29mph. Acceleration: 0-60mph 16.8sec; standing $\frac{1}{4}$-mile 20.1sec. Acceleration in gears: top, 20-40mph 11.7sec/50-70mph 15.1sec; third, 20-40mph 7.0sec/40-60mph 9.1sec. Fuel consumption: 28 to 36mpg (Imperial).

1071cc Mini-Cooper S, produced 1963 and 1964

Type designation	Austin Mini-Cooper 1071S/Morris Mini-Cooper 1071S
Built	Longbridge, Birmingham
Numbers manufactured	4,017

Basic style, design and layout, as for original 997 Mini-Cooper except for following technical differences

Engine	Bore, stroke and capacity 70.6 x 68.26mm, (2.80 x 2.69in) 1071cc(65.35cu. in); 9.0:1 compression ratio. Maximum power 70bhp (net) at 6000rpm. Maximum torque 62lb.ft at 4500rpm.
Chassis	Track (front) 4ft. 0.6in (123.3cm) Track (rear) 3ft 11.3in (120.2cm)
Brakes	Front disc 7.5in. diameter. Vacuum servo assistance standard.
Wheels and tyres	Optional 4.5in rim width; 145-10in. radial ply tyres.
Construction	Unladen weight (approx) 1410lb (640kg).
Electrical system	12 volt, 43amp battery.
Performance	Source *Motor* 1963. Maximum speed 95mph. Maximum speeds in gears, 3rd gear 84mph; 2nd gear 62mph, 1st gear 37mph. Acceleration: 0-60mph 12.9sec; standing $\frac{1}{4}$-mile 18.9sec. Acceleration in gears: top, 20-40mph 10.4sec/50-70mph 12.1sec; third, 20-40mph 6.7sec/50-70mph 8.2sec. Fuel consumption: 26 to 40mpg (Imperial).

970cc Mini-Cooper S, produced 1964 and 1965

Type designation	Austin Mini-Cooper 970S/Morris Mini-Cooper 970S
Built	Longbridge, Birmingham
Numbers manufactured	972

Basic style, design and layout as for 1071S model except for following technical differences.

Engine	Bore, stroke and capacity 70.6 x 61.91mm (2.80 x 2.44in), 970cc (59.2cu.in); 9.75:1 compression ratio. Maximum power 65bhp (net) at 6500rpm. Maximum torque 55lb.ft at 3500rpm.
Suspension	From September 1964, Hydrolastic suspension units, with front-rear interconnection, superseded rubber cone springs.
Performance	No independently authenticated sets of performances figures were ever made available.

1275cc Mini-Cooper S, produced 1964 to 1971

Type designation   Austin Mini-Cooper 1275S/Morris Mini-Cooper 1275S

Built   Longbridge, Birmingham

Numbers manufactured   40,449

Basic style, design and layout as for 1071S model except for following technical differences.

Engine   Bore, stroke and capacity 70.6 x 81.28mm (2.80 x 3.20in), 1275cc (77.8cu.in); 9.5:1 compression ratio. Maximum power 76bhp (net) at 5800rpm. Maximum torque 79lbf. ft. at 3000rpm.

Transmission   At first, overall gear ratios 11.02, 6.60, 4.62, 3.44. reverse 11.02:1, without synchromesh on first gear. Final drive ratio 3.44:1.
During 1968 (date not known), all-synchromesh gearbox was fitted with following overall ratios: 11.35, 7.13, 4.65, 3.44; reverse 11.52:1.

Suspension   From September 1964, Hydrolastic suspension units, with front-rear interconnection, superseded rubber cone springs.

Bodywork   From October 1967, MkII model, with larger rear window, revised trim, badging and details, introduced.
From March 1970, MkIII model, no longer Austin or Morris, but plain Mini, with wind-up door windows, concealed hinges for doors, different seats and trim, introduced.

Fuel system   From January 1966, twin fuel tanks of 11 gallons (50 litres) standardised.

Performance   Source *Motor* 1964. Maximum speed 97mph. Maximum speeds in gears: 3rd gear 75mph; 2nd gear 52mph, 1st gear 31mph. Acceleration: 0-60mph 10.9sec; standing $\frac{1}{4}$-mile 18.2sec. Acceleration in gears: top, 20-40mph 7.6sec/50-70mph 9.2sec; third, 20-40mph 5.1sec/50-70mph 7sec. Fuel consumption: 28 to 36mpg (Imperial).

ROAD TESTS

THE MOTOR   September 20 1961

The Motor Road Test No. 35/61

Make: Morris   **Type:** Mini-Cooper.
Makers: Morris Motors, Ltd., Cowley, Oxford.

Test Data

World copyright reserved; no unauthorized reproduction in whole or in part.

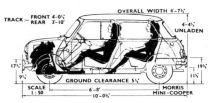

CONDITIONS: Weather: Dry and hot with slight breeze. (Temperature 66°-77°F., Barometer 29.8 in. Hg.) Surface: Dry concrete and tarred macadam. Fuel: Premium-grade pump petrol (approx. 97 Research Method Octane Rating).

INSTRUMENTS

Speedometer at 30 m.p.h.	..	..	3% fast
Speedometer at 60 m.p.h.	..	..	1% slow
Speedometer at 80 m.p.h.	..	..	1% slow
Distance recorder ..	..	..	1% slow

WEIGHT

Kerb weight (unladen, but with oil coolant and fuel for approx. 50 miles) .. 12¼ cwt.
Front/rear distribution of kerb weight .. 63/37
Weight laden as tested .. .. .. 16¼ cwt.

MAXIMUM SPEEDS

Mean lap speed around banked circuit 85.2 m.p.h.
Best one way -mile time equals. 84.1 m.p.h.

"Maximile" speed. (Timed quarter mile after one mile accelerating from rest.)
Mean of opposite runs .. .. 82.3 m.p.h.
Best one-way time equals .. 84.1 m.p.h.

Speed in gears. (Limits indicated on speedometer.)
Speed in 3rd. gear .. .. .. .63 m.p.h.
Speed in 2nd. gear .. .. .. .46 m.p.h.
Speed in 1st gear .. .. .. 28 m.p.h.

FUEL CONSUMPTION

56.5 m.p.g. at constant 30 m.p.h. on level.
53.0 m.p.g. at constant 40 m.p.h. on level.
47.0 m.p.g. at constant 50 m.p.h. on level.
41.0 m.p.g. at constant 60 m.p.h. on level.
34.5 m.p.g. at constant 70 m.p.h. on level.
27.0 m.p.g. at constant 80 m.p.h. on level.
22.0 m.p.g. at maximum speed of approx. 85 m.p.h. on level.

Overall Fuel Consumption for 1,064 miles, 30.75 gallons, equals 34.6 m.p.g. (8.15 litres/100 km.)

Touring Fuel Consumption (m.p.g. at steady speed midway between 30 m.p.h. and maximum, less 5% allowance for acceleration) 40.5 m.p.g.
Fuel tank capacity (makers' figure) 5¼ gallons.

STEERING

Turning circle between kerbs:
left .. 31¼ ft. right .. 29¾ ft.
Turns of steering wheel from lock to lock 2¼

BRAKES from 30 m.p.h. (tested when warm, see text)

0.90 g retardation (equivalent to 33⅓ ft. stopping distance) with 90 lb. pedal pressure.
0.80 g retardation (equivalent to 37½ ft. stopping distance) with 75 lb. pedal pressure.
0.56 g retardation (equivalent to 54 ft. stopping distance) with 50 lb. pedal pressure.
0.25 g retardation (equivalent to 120 ft. stopping distance) with 25 lb. pedal pressure.

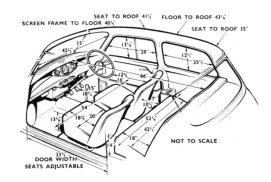

SEATS ADJUSTABLE   **NOT TO SCALE**

ACCELERATION TIMES from standstill			
0-30 m.p.h.	..	..	4.8 sec.
0-40 m.p.h.	..	..	7.7 sec.
0-50 m.p.h.	..	..	11.8 sec.
0-60 m.p.h.	..	..	17.2 sec.
0-70 m.p.h.	..	..	26.3 sec.
0-80 m.p.h.	..	..	47.3 sec.
Standing quarter mile	..	..	21.1 sec.

ACCELERATION TIMES on upper ratios	Top gear	3rd gear
10-30 m.p.h.	10.7 sec.	7.4 sec.
20-40 m.p.h.	11.8 sec.	7.6 sec.
30-50 m.p.h.	12.7 sec.	7.9 sec.
40-60 m.p.h.	13.3 sec.	9.4 sec.
50-70 m.p.h.	16.5 sec.	—
60-80 m.p.h.	30.6 sec.	—

HILL CLIMBING at sustained steady speeds

Max. gradient on top gear .. .. 1 in 12.4 (Tapley 180 lb./ton)
Max. gradient on 3rd gear .. .. 1 in 7.5 (Tapley 295 lb./ton)
Max. gradient on 2nd gear .. .. 1 in 5.3 (Tapley 415 lb./ton)

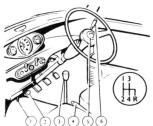

1, Heater shutter. 2, Dip switch. 3, Gear lever. 4, Handbrake. 5, Horn button. 6, Direction indicator switch and warning light. 7, Windscreen washer button. 8, Heater temperature control. 9, Wiper switch. 10, Ignition and starter key. 11, Heater fan switch. 12, Fuel gauge. 13, Lights switch. 14, Fresh air heater intake control. 15, Choke. 16, Water temperature gauge. 17, Main beam warning light. 18, Oil pressure warning light. 19, Speedometer. 20, Dynamo charge warning light. 21, Oil pressure gauge. 22, Panel light switch.

THE MOTOR   September 20 1961

The Morris Mini-Cooper

New duo-tone colour schemes, a chromium-plated grille and the Morris Cooper motif are the only exterior features which distinguish this from standard Mini-Minors.   A description of the new car will be found on pages 257-259.

A Wolf Cub in Sheep's Clothing

AS one of the world's most compact genuine four-seat cars, the Morris Mini-Minor is famous also for its immensely responsive steering. When the name Cooper is added to its title, the Mini-Minor justifies identification with the builders of world championship-winning Grand Prix cars by having a larger and more sporting engine, close-ratio gears and disc front brakes which lift its road performance into an even higher class. With a top speed of just over 85 m.p.h.. and effortless top gear acceleration such as one associates with

considerably larger cars as well as very quick acceleration when the gears are used. the "Mini" becomes an extremely rapid car on ordinary give-and-take roads.

First impressions are not of a sporting car, however, but of a compact yet roomy saloon which is much more "de luxe" in its furnishing than the majority of small cars. Upholstery has been smartened up. and the washable plastic roof lining now carries a proper interior lamp: the centrally placed instrument nacelle has been widened to accommodate a thermometer and oil pressure

gauge although it remains rather remote from the driver's normal sight line and. after dark, only the speedometer and fuel contents gauge are illuminated. Less conspicuous improvements are also welcome. sliding windows in the doors having much more satisfactory catches than were fitted to early Mini-Minors (although the hinged rear quarter windows are still liable to blow shut at high cruising speeds. blowing open again when a door is slammed!) and the starter operating from the ignition key instead of from a button. Availability of a fresh-air interior

Oil pressure and water temperature gauges supplement the improved centrally mounted speedometer dial. Better upholstery and a remote control gear lever are also standard features.

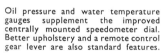

In Brief

Price £465, plus purchase tax £214 7s. 3d. equals £679 7s. 3d.	
Capacity	997 c.c.
Unladen kerb weight ..	12½ cwt.
Acceleration :	
20-40 m.p.h. in top gear ..	11.8 sec.
0-50 m.p.h. through gears	11.8 sec.
Maximum top gear gradient 1 in 12.4.	
Maximum speed	85.2 m.p.h.
"Maximile" speed	82.3 m.p.h.
Touring fuel consumption ..	40.5 m.p.g.
Gearing : 14.9 m.p.h. in top gear at 1,000 r.p.m.; 27.4 m.p.h. at 1,000 ft./min. piston speed.	

THE MOTOR   September 20 1961

The Morris Mini-Cooper

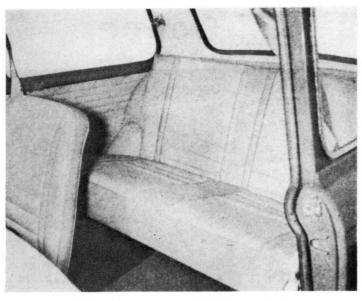

Despite the car's small overall size, there is ample room for two large adults in the back seat. Pillar- and floor-mounted safety straps are an option for front seat passengers.

heater brings a welcome end to misting-up dangers in humid weather, although on our test car the push-pull cable operation of its hot water valve failed. A carpeted floor in the luggage locker is another improvement, especially as this floor over the spare wheel can readily be removed for special occasions when every possible cubic inch of space is required.

Such refinements as these emphasize that the Mini-Cooper is not a racing Mini-Minor, but a better all-round car than the lower-priced versions which preceded (and of course continue in production alongside) it. Engine tuning alone could have given power at high r.p.m., but the long-stroke crankshaft which increases engine displacement from 848 c.c. to 997 c.c. also gives such figures as top gear acceleration from 20 to 40 m.p.h. in only 11.8 sec. That sort of urge in top gear, and ability to exceed 85 m.p.h. on the level, would be highly satisfactory for a conventional saloon car of 2-litre engine size.

A moderate degree of tune has been applied to the engine, although it will still run on premium petrol without demanding " 100 octane " fuel. Our test model had a lumpy and rather fast tick-over, perhaps partly due to the special camshaft which lets it breathe well at high r.p.m., but not helped by awkward access to two S.U. carburetters, adjuster screws on which have only the feeblest springs to discourage them rotating as the engine vibrates. A very real advantage of this twin-carburetter long-stroke engine was its willingness to pull smoothly and hard almost immediately after a start from cold, and although at low cruising speeds it uses slightly more fuel than the smaller single-carburetter

A longer-throw crankshaft has increased the capacity of the B.M.C. A-series engine to 997 c.c. With a special camshaft and twin S.U. carburetters, it gives genuine 85 m.p.h. performance.

engine, overall petrol economy is excellent for such a roomy and lively car.

Welcome though its " big car " ability to overtake or sweep easily up hills in top gear may be, this version of the Mini-Minor also has closer spacing of its four gearbox ratios. Marks on the speedometer dial which it seems purposeless to over-step suggest maxima of approximately 65 m.p.h. in 3rd gear, 45 m.p.h. in 2nd gear and nearly 30 m.p.h. in 1st gear, these being the change-up speeds used when recording (with two men and some heavy test equipment aboard) such figures as from rest to 50 m.p.h. in 11.8 sec. and to 70 m.p.h. in 26.3 sec.

Adoption of the traditional sports car remote control brings this model's gear lever to a very convenient position, but with the transverse engine and front-wheel drive involves mechanical complexities. The gear control is very

satisfactorily positive, but after some 3,000 miles was still heavy to use on our test car; synchromesh is provided on the upper three gears, and although better than hitherto it remains rather easy to override. Despite the high bottom gear, restarting with two or three people in the car is possible on a 1 in 4 hill, and the handbrake holds securely on even steeper gradients if pulled up with reasonable firmness.

An exhaust note which is business-like but not aggressive, a new 16-blade fan to push air transversely through the radiator, and widespread use of sound-absorbing material make this model at least as quiet as earlier Mini-Minors and at times usefully quieter. It can cruise very effortlessly at 70 m.p.h. or more, but when driven hard it reminds one, by appreciable power roar and road rumble augmented by general fussiness towards the maximum speeds in the lower gears, that this is a small and light car. It is obviously unfair, but given a small saloon which performs like larger models costing perhaps twice as much, one tends to expect also the refinement of a much heavier and more cumbersome vehicle.

Nothing could be less cumbersome than a Mini-Minor, and either by chance or thanks to the nylon tyres fitted to Cooper models, our test car seemed more than normally responsive to a light touch on its steering. One cannot say that it is anything but stable, yet it takes very very little steering movement to swing the Mini-Cooper round an obstacle during fast driving. Taken into a corner as fast as seems safe or a little faster, this little saloon claws its way round with a good deal of " drift " but a notably stubborn reluctance to spin or run out of road. More power means that the effect normal to front-wheel-driven cars (which, if the accelerator pedal is released whilst cornering, self-centre their steering less strongly and show less understeer) is a little more evident, but it never seems to become embarrassing.

By 1961 standards Mini-Minors have unusually firm suspension, but damping is gentle and the progressiveness of rubber springs is such that one cannot ever detect a bump stop coming into harsh

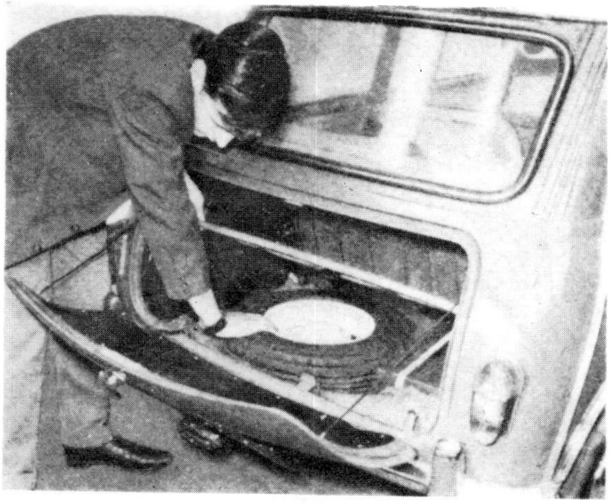

A carpeted floor over the spare wheel can be removed if extra luggage space is needed.

action. On a secondary road the ride can be lively, but it is shock free and has no exaggerated movements such as can induce car-sickness in more softly sprung vehicles—major humps or hollows which worry some soft-riding cars are almost totally ignored. Riding comfort seems just as good in the back seat as in front.

Application of disc brakes to the front wheels has certainly achieved the desired result of eliminating fade in severe conditions. Several stops from 60 m.p.h. or more, made in a quick series, can produce a smell of hot brakes as large amounts of energy are dissipated, but instead of their effectiveness fading the brakes then become rather more responsive to moderate pedal pressures. In utter contrast to what has been normal, the one circumstance which can require an embarrassingly large pedal effort to bring the wheels close to locking is the need to make an emergency stop when the brakes are completely cold as a result of the pedal having remained untouched during a good many miles.

Whilst some people who have not yet experienced it for themselves are still incredulous concerning the very large amount of passenger space which can exist in a car only 10 ft. 0½ in. long, most keen motorists know what a miracle has been performed by banishing the engine and gearbox to a tight-packed spot at the very front of the body and putting four tiny wheels at the extreme corners of the car. Hollowed-out doors and body sides provide unrestricted elbow room, above four capacious parcel compartments which cannot be insulted with the name "pockets"—there is also a facia shelf and plenty of parcel space under the rear seat.

Men with very long legs will usually criticize both the range of driving-seat adjustment and the forward-crouch driving position, but can in fact drive long distances in reasonable comfort and have room for two adult passengers behind them. Small pedals are spaced widely enough to accommodate broad shoes, yet not so far apart as to rule out intentional toe-and-heel operation of brake and accelerator simultaneously. Sliding windows, when combined with a fresh-air heater which can be set to admit unheated air to the body, provide reasonably draught-free ventilation. Rigid door handles in place of pull-straps are an orthodoxy which pleases passengers, even though handles at the rear extremities of front-hinged doors are less accessible than were the straps.

The ability of ordinary Morris Mini-Minors to make fast point-to-point progress on far from perfect roads is by now a very widely observed phenomenon. With maximum and cruising speeds raised by 10-15 m.p.h. and much-improved acceleration, this Cooper version of Alec Issigonis' remarkable design is even faster, its higher 3rd gear being especially welcome for overtaking more promptly and safely.

This is the fastest production saloon car of its size ever to figure in our regular series of Road Test Reports. So much performance, combined with a lot of practical merit and quite a high standard of refinement, will obviously make many people decide that a sum of about £680 is better spent on this model than on something bigger but no better.

The World Copyright of this article and illustrations is strictly reserved © Temple Press Limited, 1961.

Specification

Engine

Cylinders	4 (Transversely mounted engine)
Bore	62.43 mm.
Stroke	81.28 mm.
Cubic capacity	997 c.c.
Piston area	18.96 sq. in.
Valves	In-line o h.v. (pushrods)
Compression ratio	9/1
Carburetter	2 S.U. inclined, type HS2
Fuel pump	S.U. electrical below fuel tank
Ignition timing control	Centrifugal and vacuum
Oil filter	Purolator full-flow
Max. power	55 b.h.p. at 6,000 r.p.m.
Piston speed at max. b.h.p.	3,200 ft./min

Transmission

Clutch	B.M.C. 7⅛ in. single dry plate
Top gear (s/m)	3.765
3rd gear (s/m)	5.11
2nd gear (s/m)	7.21
1st gear	12.05
Reverse	12.05
Front wheel driving shafts	Birfield with constant velocity outer universals
Final drive	Helical gears from transverse gearbox
Top gear m.p.h. at 1,000 r.p.m.	14.9
Top gear m.p.h. at 1,000 ft./min. piston speed	27.4

Chassis

Brakes	Lockheed hydraulic, discs at front with two-ratio pressure booster valve, drums at rear with pressure limiting valve.
Brake dimensions	Front discs 7 in. dia.; rear drums 7 in. dia. × 1¼ in. wide
Friction areas	45 sq. in. of lining area working on 157.4 sq. in. rubbed area of discs and drums.
Suspension: Front	Independent by transverse wishbones and Moulton rubber springs
Suspension: Rear	Independent by trailing arms and Moulton rubber springs
Shock Absorbers	Telescopic (orifice type)
Steering gear	Rack and pinion
Tyres	Dunlop Gold Seal nylon tubeless, 5.20-10

Coachwork and Equipment

Starting handle	None
Battery mounting	Under luggage locker floor
Jack	Pillar type
Jacking points	Under sides of body
Standard tool kit	Jack, wheelbrace sparking plug spanner and tommy bar
Exterior lights	2 headlamps with pilot bulbs, 2 stop/tail lamps, rear number plate lamp.
Number of electrical fuses	2
Direction indicators	Amber flashers, self-cancelling
Windscreen wipers	Twin-blade electrical, non self-parking
Windscreen washers	Pump-type
Sun visors	Two, hinge mounted
Instruments	Speedometer with non-decimal total mileage recorder, fuel contents gauge, oil pressure gauge, coolant thermometer
Warning lights	Dynamo charge, headlamp main beam, turn indicators
Locks	With ignition key. Ignition/starter switch, driver's door, luggage locker
Glove lockers	None
Map pockets	Wide compartments in two doors and on each side of rear seat
Parcel shelves	Full-width on facia
Ashtrays	1 front, 2 rear
Cigar lighters	None
Interior lights	One in roof (manual switch only)
Interior heater	Smiths recirculatory heater and demister. (Fresh-air type optional extra)
Car radio	Radiomobile as optional extra
Extras available	Fresh-air heater, radio
Upholstery material	Leathercloth
Floor covering	Pile carpet with underfelt
Exterior colours standardized	Six duotone combinations
Alternative body styles	None (lower-powered engine etc., available in same body)

Maintenance

Sump and transmission	8 pints plus 1 pint in filter S.A.E. 30 engine oil above freezing or S.A.E. 20W down to 10 F.
Gearbox and final drive lubricated from engine.	
Steering gear lubricant	S.A.E. 90 hypoid gear oil
Cooling system capacity	5¼ pints plus 1 pint in optional heater (2 drain taps)
Chassis lubrication	By grease gun every 1,000 miles to 10 points
Ignition timing	T.d.c. static
Contact-breaker gap	0.014-0.016
Sparking plug type	Champion N5
Sparking plug gap	0.024-0.026 in.
Valve timing	Inlet opens 16° before t.d.c. and closes 56° after b.d.c.; Exhaust opens 51° before b.d.c. and closes 21° after t.d.c.
Tappet clearances (hot or cold)	Inlet and exhaust 0.012 in
Front wheel toe-out	⅛ in.
Camber angle	1° normally laden
Castor angle	1½° normally laden
Steering swivel pin inclination	9½° normally laden
Tyre pressures	Front 24 lb. Rear 22 lb.
Brake fluid	Lockheed (S.A.E. Spec. 70-R-1)
Battery	Lucas GLTW7A, 12 volt 34 amp. hr
Miscellaneous	Top up carburetter dashpots with S.A.E. 20 engine oil

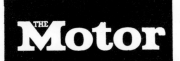

THE MOTOR April 24 1963

MAKE: Morris *TYPE: Mini-Cooper S*
MAKERS: British Motor Corporation Limited, Longbridge, Birmingham

The Motor

ROAD TEST ● No. 16/63

TEST DATA:

CONDITIONS: *Weather: Mild with light wind (10 m.p.h.) and intermittent rain. (Temperature 45°-50°F., Barometer 29·8 in Hg.) Surface: Damp during acceleration tests; otherwise dry. Fuel: Premium grade pump petrol (98 Octane by Research Method).*

MAXIMUM SPEEDS

Mean lap speed around banked circuit	94·5 m.p.h.
Best one-way ¼-mile time equals	98·9 m.p.h.

"Maximile" Speed (Timed quarter mile after one mile accelerating from rest)

Mean of opposite runs	91·8 m.p.h.
Best one-way time equals	93·8 m.p.h.

Speed in gears

Max. speed in 3rd gear	84 m.p.h.
Max. speed in 2nd gear	62 m.p.h.
Max. speed in 1st gear	37 m.p.h.

ACCELERATION TIMES from standstill

0-30 m.p.h.	4·0 sec.
0-40 m.p.h.	6·9 sec.
0-50 m.p.h.	9·0 sec.
0-60 m.p.h.	12·9 sec.
0-70 m.p.h.	17·1 sec.
0-80 m.p.h.	23·2 sec.
0-90 m.p.h.	40·1 sec.
Standing quarter mile	18·9 sec.

ACCELERATION TIMES on upper ratios

	Top gear	Third gear
10-30 m.p.h.	11·6 sec.	7·9 sec.
20-40 m.p.h.	10·4 sec.	6·7 sec.
30-50 m.p.h.	11·0 sec.	7·0 sec.
40-60 m.p.h.	10·8 sec.	7·2 sec.
50-70 m.p.h.	12·1 sec.	8·2 sec.
60-80 m.p.h.	16·0 sec.	10·7 sec.
70-90 m.p.h.	26·4 sec.	—

HILL CLIMBING

Max. gradient climbable at steady speed.

Top gear	1 in 10·1 (Tapley 220 lb./ton)
3rd gear	1 in 6·4 (Tapley 345 lb./ton)
2nd gear	1 in 4·4 (Tapley 495 lb./ton)

FUEL CONSUMPTION

Overall Fuel Consumption for 1,345 miles, 50¼ gallons, equals 26·8 m.p.g. (10·55 litres/100 km.)

Touring Fuel Consumption (m.p.g. at steady speed midway between 30 m.p.h. and maximum, less 5% allowance for acceleration) 39·5 m.p.g.

Fuel tank capacity (maker's figure) 5½ gallons

Direct top gear

57½ m.p.g.	at constant 30 m.p.h. on level
54½ m.p.g.	at constant 40 m.p.h. on level
50½ m.p.g.	at constant 50 m.p.h. on level
42½ m.p.g.	at constant 60 m.p.h. on level
38½ m.p.g.	at constant 70 m.p.h. on level
32 m.p.g.	at constant 80 m.p.h. on level
21½ m.p.g.	at constant 90 m.p.h. on level

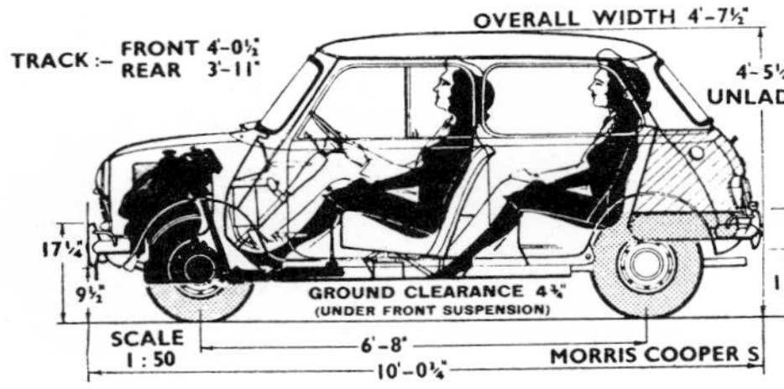
OVERALL WIDTH 4'-7½"
TRACK :- FRONT 4'-0⅝" REAR 3'-11"
4'-5¼" UNLADEN
17¼"
9½"
19¼"
11½"
GROUND CLEARANCE 4⅜"
(UNDER FRONT SUSPENSION)
SCALE 1 : 50
6'-8"
10'-0¼"
MORRIS COOPER S

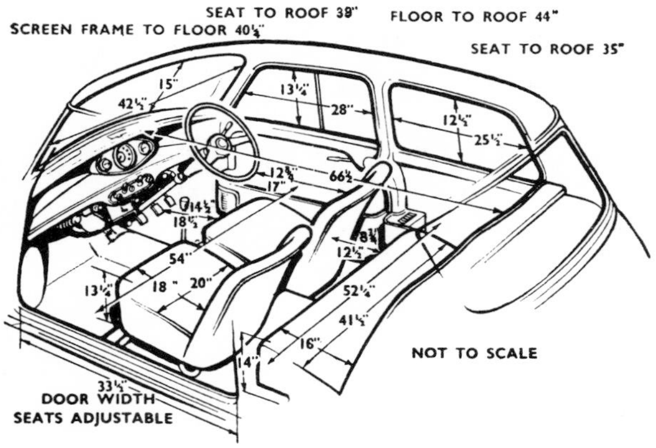
SEAT TO ROOF 38"
FLOOR TO ROOF 44"
SCREEN FRAME TO FLOOR 40¾"
SEAT TO ROOF 35"
15"
42½"
13½"
28"
12½"
25½"
66½"
17"
54"
18"
20"
52¼"
41½"
16"
14"
33½"
DOOR WIDTH
SEATS ADJUSTABLE
NOT TO SCALE

BRAKES

Deceleration and equivalent s opping distance from 30 m.p.h.

1·00 g with 60 lb. pedal pressure	(30 ft.)
·71 g with 50 lb. pedal pressure	(42 ft.)
·37 g with 25 lb. pedal pressure	(81 ft.)

STEERING

Turning circle between kerbs:

Left	31¾ft.
Right	29 ft.
Turns of steering wheel from lock to lock	2½

INSTRUMENTS

Speedometer at 30 m.p.h.	3% fast
Speedometer at 60 m.p.h.	accurate
Speedometer at 90 m.p.h.	3% fast
Distance recorder	2½% fast

WEIGHT

Kerb weight (unladen, but with oil, coolant and fuel for approximately 50 miles)	13 cwt.
Front/rear distribution of kerb weight	63/37
Weight laden as tested	16¼ cwt.

Specification

Engine

Cylinders	4
Bore	70·6 mm.
Stroke	68·26 mm.
Cubic capacity	1,071 c.c.
Piston area	24·3 sq. in.
Valves	Overhead (pushrod)
Compression ratio	9/1
Carburetters	Twin S.U. Type HS2
Fuel pump	S.U. electric
Ignition timing control	Centrifugal and vacuum
Oil filter	External full flow
Maximum power (net)	70 b.h.p.
at	6,000 r.p.m.
Maximum torque (net)	62 lb. ft.
at	4,500 r.p.m.
Piston speed at maximum b.h.p.	2,690 ft./min.

Transmission

Clutch	BMC, 7¼ in. single dry plate
Top gear	3·765
3rd gear	5·109
2nd gear	7·213
1st gear	12·047
Reverse	12.047
Final drive	Helical gears from transverse gearbox
Top gear m.p.h. at 1,000 r.p.m.	14·7
Top gear m.p.h. at 1,000 ft./min. piston speed	32·8

Chassis

Brakes: Lockheed hydraulic; disc front, drum rear, with Hydrovac servo

Brake dimensions:
Front discs .. 7½ in. dia.
Rear drums, 7 in. dia. × 1¼ in. wide

Friction areas 51 sq. in. of friction lining (17·3 front, 33·7 rear) operating on 179 sq. in. swept area of discs and drums

Suspension:
Front: Independent by rubber springs and transverse wishbones. Rear: Independent by rubber springs and trailing arms.

Shock absorbers:

Front	Telescopic hydraulic
Rear	Telescopic hydraulic
Steering gear:	Rack and pinion
Tyres:	Dunlop SP 145—10 (5·5—10) (Dunlop C41 optional)

Morris Cooper S

A FEW years ago the idea of any Morris or Austin being eligible for competition work as it stood would have seemed fantastic. Yet today the homely-looking Mini-Cooper is one of the most respected performers in saloon car racing and rallies.

Testing the Mini-Cooper in its 997 c.c. 55 b.h.p. road form when it first appeared in the autumn of 1961, *The Motor* called it "a wolf cub in sheep's clothing." The new S type competition version, capping that performance substantially, surely rates as a full-grown wolf, in potentialities if not size. Thanks to a 1,071 c.c. engine embodying many features of the B.M.C. Formula Junior racing engine and giving 15 more b.h.p. than the normal Mini-Cooper, the maximum speed is nearly

10 m.p.h. up at 94.5 m.p.h. and 0–50 m.p.h. acceleration is 9.0 sec. as against 11.8 sec. The performance, moreover, is controlled by remarkable braking power.

Although the engine in this state of tune makes itself both felt and heard, the car is completely tractable, giving as good a service for shopping on Saturday morning as when racing on the Silverstone club circuit in the afternoon or rallying the same night. At a price of under £700 inclusive of Purchase Tax, this is one of the most inexpensive, most versatile and most exhilarating road cars ever offered.

How it does it

THE S type engine retains the 68.26 mm. stroke of the standard A-series Mini engine, but the bore is enlarged from 62.43 mm. to 70.6 mm., by making the centres of Nos. 2 and 3 cylinders ¼ in. closer, and the outer pairs ¼ in. wider apart. Sturdier but lighter connecting rods have offset little ends, the main and big-end bearings are of indium-infused

Little innocent: only an 'S' above the nameplate, and the perforated wheels carrying Dunlop SP tyres betray the "wolf in sheep's clothing" character of B.M.C.'s latest high performance Mini variant.

In Brief

Price (as tested) £575 plus purchase tax £120 7s. 1d. equals £695 7s. 1d.

Capacity	1,071 c.c.
Unladen kerb weight	13 cwt.
Acceleration:	
20–40 m.p.h. in top gear	10.4 sec.
0–50 m.p.h. through gears	9.0 sec.
Maximum top gear gradient	1 in 10.1
Maximum speed	94.5 m.p.h.
Overall fuel consumption	26.8 m.p.g.
Touring fuel consumption	39.5 m.p.g.
Gearing: 14.7 m.p.h. in top gear at 1,000 r.p.m.	

Instruments (*right*). The Mini-Cooper S has only three dials: a 120 m.p.h. speedometer with fuel gauge and mileage recorder, flanked by oil pressure and water temperature gauges. The new fresh air heater below the parcels shelf is now standard equipment on all Mini-Coopers.

Furnishings (*below*) include Vynide seating and carpeted floor, with no tunnel to restrict leg space in the back.

Stout heart (*below right*) of the S is this 1,071 c.c., 70 b.h.p., twin-carburetter version of B.M.C.'s famous A series pushrod o.h.v. engine. The brake servo can be seen on the left, below the heater duct.

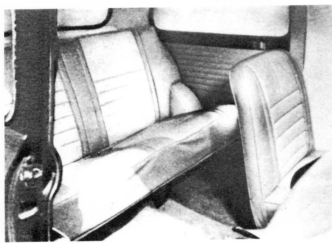

Morris Cooper S

copper lead, and are now both of 2 in. diameter, and a stiffer nitrided crankshaft in EN 40B high-tensile steel is used. Forged steel rockers replace the normal fabricated type, while Stellite-tipped valves in Nimonic 80 are used, working in copper-nickel alloy guides.

As tested, the S had standard Mini-Cooper gear ratios and a 3.76 to 1 final drive, but a choice of closer ratios is available and also a 3.44/1 final drive. Second and third mainshaft gears run in needle rollers, and the 7¼ in. diameter clutch has bonded linings to withstand the extra torque. All these, and other subtle changes are a direct inheritance of racing experience in the saloon and Formula Junior classes. The rest of the car, too, reflects such experience.

Lockheed front disc brakes are increased by ⅛ in. diameter to 7¼ in., and by ⅛ in. in thickness to ⅜ in.; larger brake pads are also fitted, with a material gain in friction lining area, cooling area and thermal storage capacity, and a Hydrovac servo booster greatly reduces the required pedal pressure, giving extremely powerful braking. The well-known ADO 15 rubber suspension at front and rear is unchanged and Dunlop SP tyres are fitted as standard.

What it does

THE Mini-Cooper S is undoubtedly an extremely fast car under any road conditions. It can whip through heavy town traffic, traverse twisting, hilly roads at a fine gait, and cruise at 90 m.p.h. on the motorway. Starting is immediate, and choke is required for a short while only, after which the car is smooth, tractable and well-mannered at low speeds, quite suitable to go shopping in. Yet its speed and accelerative

qualities will seriously disrupt the complacency of many owners of sports cars and big-engined saloons, especially as it is coupled with equally quick handling qualities and Mini manoeuvrability.

On the test car, a mean maximum speed of 94.5 m.p.h., and a best one-way quarter mile with a favourable wind of 98.9 m.p.h. were achieved. These are remarkable figures for a 1,100 c.c. saloon car capable of comfortably seating four people, and the acceleration is equally striking. From a standstill, 30 m.p.h. takes just 4 sec., 0-60 m.p.h. is achieved in 12.9 sec., and 0-80 m.p.h. in 25.2 sec.

The performance has to be paid for somehow. Seventy brake horsepower from a small engine of "cooking" origin means a high degree of tune and a busy power unit. The test car developed a tendency to stall in traffic, remedied temporarily by occasional blipping of the throttle to prevent the rather rich mixture "ganging up" in the inlet manifold and eventually by adjustment to the carburetters, but the throttle linkage allowed a very variable idling speed. Although flexible enough at low speeds, the engine gets progressively happier as the revs rise.

At the absolute maximum of 62 m.p.h. in second gear, and 84 m.p.h. in third, vibration was carried through the gear lever to an uncomfortable extent. Although the engine note is taut and purposeful on brief acquaintance, the regular motorway traveller might soon tire of it at high speed, were it not for other compensations. Regrettably, no rev counter is fitted as standard, and gearchange points at 30, 50 and 70, which can be well exceeded, are marked in yellow on the 120 m.p.h. speedometer.

Fuel consumption, too, is naturally heavier at 26.8 m.p.g. than the normal Mini-Cooper's 34.6 m.p.g., but the gentler driver is rewarded by a touring consumption as high as 39.5 m.p.g. Engine oil on the hard-used test car was burnt at the rate of 135 miles per pint, a consumption attributable partly to the fact that the chrome scraper rings do not bed in very quickly, partly to the use of a larger capacity oil pump and enlarged oilways to ensure adequate lubrication under the

THE MOTOR   April 24 1963

stress of competition, and partly to the continual use of very high r.p.m.

How it handles

WITH so much power under the throttle foot, good road-holding and steering are essential, and the Mini system copes admirably. Use of the front drive "throttle-on" technique enables corners to be taken at remarkable speed, and although it proved possible to spin the wheels on tight, fast turns, the car remained controllable at all times. The light, high-geared rack and pinion steering with its immediate "feel" and response contribute vitally to the excellent handling and controllability, as do the braced tread Dunlop SP tyres on wheels which have rims one inch wider than normal. This combination gives extremely high cornering power and a rapidity of response to the steering which can make cornering rather jerky until a driver strange to the car acquires the necessary lightness of touch. When he does he finds that cornering limits are so high, both in the wet and the dry, that they are difficult to explore; there is no tyre squeal and these special tyres, used for some time on B.M.C. rally cars, reduce considerably the drift angles on bends and, in consequence, reduce also the usual change in handling between "throttle on" and "throttle off" conditions which becomes almost imperceptible when one is trying extremely hard.

The ratios of the four-speed gearbox are excellent for all-

round road use, and the remote-control gear lever is easy to reach. There is no synchromesh on first gear, which is an occasional inconvenience with an engine thriving on high revs. On the comparatively new test car, gear lever movement was a little stiff, while shopping drivers may not relish the fairly heavy clutch pedal pressure.

The braking powers of the S are formidable, and in complete harmony with its performance. The disc-front, drum-rear combination allied to Hydrovac servo assistance gives extremely effective braking with only gentle pedal pressure, while repeated use brought no evidence of brake fade. The "velvet touch" proved particularly necessary in the wet when over-hard application brought considerable initial pull until the discs dried off. An emergency stop from about 70 m.p.h. on dry roads, however, pulled the car up virtually all-square, with the slightest hint of wheel lock on the nearside.

During the test the brakes developed an intermittent tendency to stick on momentarily after releasing the pedal, spoiling the cleanness of the run-down to corners in the lower gears. Apart from this, they were beyond reproach.

There is some pitch and quite a lot of bounce over bumpy surfaces, the penalty of firm springs and lack of overhang, and bumps also affect the cornering, causing some wallow and tending to throw the car off line, especially on a trailing throttle. Otherwise, rough-road handling is good, and the "van" angle of the Mini's steering column provides excellent controllability and good all-round vision as well, all of which adds to the eminent safety of the Mini-Cooper.

Furnishings and Layout

THE front seats in this B.M.C. projectile are comfortable but upright in typical Mini fashion, but taller drivers find the legroom inadequate, even with the seat set right back. Cockpit fittings are fairly sparse. Set centrally in the dash is the oval instrument panel, containing a speedometer with fuel gauge inset, oil pressure gauge on the right, and water temperature gauge on the left. An impromptu running-out of petrol accentuated the inadequacy of a mere 5½-gallon tank; the optional extra tank of the same capacity will probably be demanded by most road and all rally users.

Below the dash, left to right, are the heater, wiper, ignition, headlight and choke controls, with lower down a kind of "gear gate" control for the very effective fresh-air heater system. All these are too far from the driver, especially if he is using safety belts. There is adequate floor space in front, as is usual with Minis, capacious parcel shelves, and very useful side boxes at the base of the two doors. The wipers are non-self-parking.

The headlights, into which are embodied the parking lights, give an excellent beam for night driving, but a "flasher" on the steering column would be very useful for warning the drivers of fast cars who are unused to seeing a Mini pushing hard in the mirror. The childish bleep of the horn, too, is utterly inadequate for a fast car and the washer button is not easy to reach. For the size of the car, the carpeted boot is spacious, while extra luggage can be carried on the opened lid. The spare wheel lives below the boot floor.

In all, the Mini-Cooper S is a car of delightful Jekyll and Hyde character, with astonishing performance concealed within its unpretentious Mini-Minor skin. More than just a "two-upmanship" car, it has a truly formidable competition potential at a very moderate price.

Extra luggage (*above*) can be carried on the open boot-lid.

The S on the lid (*below*) suggests the shock the Mini-Cooper S can administer to many drivers of larger, more powerful cars.

Coachwork and Equipment

Starting handle	.. .. ..	None	
Battery mounting	.. .. ..	In boot	
Jack	.. ..	Side lifting	
Jacking points	..	One each side on body sill	
Standard tool kit:	Jack, wheel brace and jack handle, plug spanner, tommy bar.		
Exterior lights	..	Headlamps, side lamps, tail lamps	
Number of electrical fuses	.. ..	2	
Direction indicators	..	Front and rear flashers	
Windscreen wipers	..	Electric twin-blade, single speed	
Windscreen washers	..	Wingard twin-jet	

Sun visors	.. ..	2
Instruments:	Speedometer with fuel gauge and mileage recorder. Oil gauge. Water temperature gauge.	
Warning lights	..	Ignition, headlamp, main beam
Locks:		
With ignition key	..	Doors and trunk lid
Glove lockers	.. ..	None
Map pockets	..	One in each door, two behind
Parcel shelves	..	One under facia and one behind rear seat
Ashtrays	..	On top of facia, and in each companion box

Cigar lighters	.. .. ..	None
Interior lights	.. .. ..	1
Interior heater	.. Standard.	Fresh air type
Car radio	..	Radiomobile (extra)
Extras available:	Britax safety belts (anchorages provided). Extra fuel tank (5½ gals.). Oil cooler. Sump guard.	
Upholstery material:	Vynide seats. P.V.C. leather-cloth roof lining.	
Floor covering	.. .. ..	Carpet
Exterior colours standardized	..	6
Alternative body styles	.. ..	None

Maintenance

Sump and transmission	.. 8 pints Multigrade, plus 1 pint for filter
Steering gear lubricant	.. Hypoid SAE 140
Cooling system capacity:	5¼ pints, plus 1 pint for heater (2 drain taps).
Chassis lubrication:	By grease gun every 3,000 miles to 8 points.
Ignition timing	.. .. .. 3° b.t.d.c.

Contact breaker gap	.. .. .. .015 in.
Sparking plug type	Champion N5 long reach
Sparking plug gap	.. .. .025 in.
Valve timing:	Inlet opens 5° b.t.d.c. and closes 45° a.b.d.c. Exhaust opens 51° b.b.d.c. and closes 21° a.t.d.c.
Tappet clearances (cold):	Inlet .015 in. at valve. Exhaust .015 in. at valve.
Front wheel toe-out	.. .. 1/16 in.

Camber angle	.. .. 1° min.; 3° max.
Castor angle	.. .. 3° nominal
Steering swivel pin inclination	.. 9½°
Tyre pressures:	Front, 24 lb. Rear, 22 lb.
Brake fluid	.. .. Lockheed 328
Battery type and capacity	.. 12 volt Lucas, 43 amp.-hr. at 20 hr. rate

MOTOR   week ending September 5 1964

" . . . enormous fun to drive and just about the most practical toy that £750 will buy . . . "

Number 35
MOTOR TESTED
1560 MILES

1275 S MINI COOPER

PRICE
£625 plus £130 15s. 5d. purchase tax equals £755 15s. 5d.

How they run . . .

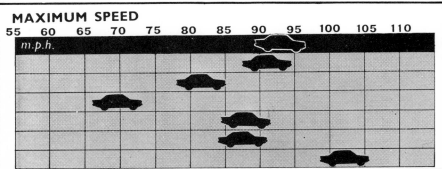

MAXIMUM SPEED

	55	60	65	70	75	80	85	90	95	100	105	110
1275S Mini Cooper £756	m.p.h.								95			
1071S Mini Cooper £695								90				
Mini Cooper £568						80						
Mini £448			65									
MG Midget £623							85					
Ford Cortina GT £749							85					
Stage 2 Triumph Spitfire £820										100		

FUEL CONSUMPTION   ● OVERALL   ○ TOURING

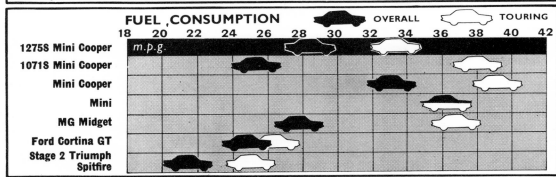

	18	20	22	24	26	28	30	32	34	36	38	40	42
1275S Mini Cooper	m.p.g.												

ACCELERATION   ● 0-50   ○ 20-40 IN TOP

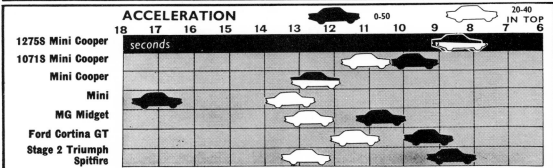

	18	17	16	15	14	13	12	11	10	9	8	7	6
1275S Mini Cooper	seconds												
1071S Mini Cooper													
Mini Cooper													
Mini													
MG Midget													
Ford Cortina GT													
Stage 2 Triumph Spitfire													

The combination of enormous torque and weight transfer can produce violent wheel spin on fierce getaways. Our test car was in Morris guise.

MINIS set their own performance standards and it is by these that we tend to judge each new specimen of the breed. In a way this is a pity because the 1275S, though probably the best Mini to date, is not the fastest of its kind we have tried. Yet judged by other production cars of comparable price, it is a truly remarkable vehicle.

The S series was developed primarily to give B.M.C. three potential winners in international racing and rallying—first in the 1,100 c.c. class and later, when the 1071S had sisters, in the 1,000 c.c. and 1,300 c.c. categories with the 970S and 1275S. To regain some of the development costs, a limited number of all three are now being sold to enthusiasts who want a competitive week-end racer and family transport all in one inexpensive package.

Even if some of the novelty has worn off, our enthusiasm for Mini motoring reached new peaks after over 1,500 miles in this car. With a maximum speed of 97 m.p.h., vivid acceleration and still further improved handling, it is enormous fun to drive and just about the most practical toy that £750 will buy. It has most of the failings of other Minis—uncomfortable seats, an awkward driving position, bumpy ride—plus some of its own like very heavy oil consumption, but the sheer delight of driving was adequate compensation for us. £2,000 will not buy a sports car that makes shorter work of cross-country journeys on indifferent roads, and, even on a motorway, this Mini can average 90 m.p.h. without apparent strain.

Performance and Economy

THE S series was developed at considerable cost to B.M.C. from the 1,100 c.c. Formula Junior racing engine used by Cooper. These engines are identical to any others in the A-series from the outside but are very different beneath the skin and their development is worth recapping to show how strength and durability have always been matched to power output.

To make the valves big enough for competition, the cylinder bore centres were moved (the outer ones out, the inner ones in). This gave standardized bore diameters of 70·64 mm., all four cylinders being " siamesed ". Differences in capacity are adjusted by the throw of the nitrided steel crankshaft, its enormous main and big-end bearings (2-in. in diameter) resisting wear through their immense surface hardness. The two smaller S engines have fashionably short strokes but the 1275 is under square with a relatively long stroke of 81·33 mm. Common to all engines are special pistons and connecting rods with extra thick gudgeon pins, substantially reshaped and larger combustion chambers

and expensive Nimonic 80 valves with Stellite stem tips to resist rocker wear. Differences in power output between the three S engines, the ex Junior and the current Formula 3 stem from camshaft design, compression ratios, manifolding and carburetters rather than capacity. Considering that the 1,000 c.c. F3 develops 90 b.h.p. with a single carburetter and the FIA's 36 mm. restrictor intake, it is clear that the twin carburetted 1275S is quite modestly stressed with an output of 75 b.h.p. at 5,800 r.p.m.—only 8 b.h.p. more than the 1071 and 10 b.h.p. more than the 970. Its potential for racing is well over 100 b.h.p.—far removed from the 28 horse-power of the original 800 c.c. engine from which the A-series was developed.

Being proportional to the extra capacity, torque output shows an appreciable improvement over the 1171S tested in April, 1963, the difference being reflected by considerably better acceleration rather than top speed. Perhaps the most remarkable figure we recorded was top gear acceleration from 10 and 30 m.p.h. in 7·8 sec.—a performance that very few cars, regardless of price or capacity, can match. We don't recommend this pointless practice but it does illustrate astonishing flexibility despite the racing ancestry.

Rev limits for the intermediate gears, marked on the speedometer at 33, 54 and 78 m.p.h. (true speeds—31, 52 and 75 m.p.h.), seem needlessly high; in the interests of maximum acceleration as well as durability, our stopwatch confirmed that it pays to change up well before these peaks (corresponding to 6,500 r.p.m.). Driving relatively gently, we were often in top well before 31 m.p.h. (1st's limit) and there was seldom need to change down for overtaking despite the 3·444 : 1 final drive—the highest of four possibles. But this is a difficult car to drive gently, its willingness and agility inspiring spirited driving just for the fun of it.

A smooth, powerful diaphragm clutch with just the right amount of feel through a rather heavy pedal makes spectacular getaways very easy; fierce release and high revs produce instant wheel spin and long black lines on the road. Interesting, but rather a waste of rubber since the best standing starts rely less on high revs and more on middle-speed torque which reaches its maximum value of 80 lb./ft. at only 3,000 r.p.m. (compared with 62 lb./ft. at 4,500 r.p.m. for the 970S). As a yardstick, the 7·7 seconds needed to reach 50 m.p.h. from rest would easily outpace an M.G. B, Mk. 10 Jaguar or 1600SC Porsche although all three have appreciably higher maximum speeds.

As most of the popular tuners can produce 100 m.p.h. Minis, we were a little disappointed with the 1275's 97 m.p.h., but in relation to other production cars, it is a remarkable speed. And, of course, the potential is much higher, almost 130 m.p.h. having been recorded by some racing versions. 100 m.p.h. can be exceeded easily downhill although at this speed the normally crisp if rather busy engine noise changes

MOTOR   week ending September 5 1964

1275 S MINI COOPER

1, brake servo. 2, starter solenoid. 3, distributor. 4, brake and clutch fluid reservoirs. 5, dip stick. 6, 1¼-in. S.U. carburetters. 7, oil filler cap. 8, windscreen washer reservoir. 9, coil. 10, radiator filler cap. The 1275S engine looks much like any other Mini from the outside: the difference is beneath the skin.

Specification

ENGINE			TRANSMISSION	
			Clutch .. .. —	
Cylinders ..	.. 4		Top gear (s/m) .. 1 : 1	
Bore and stroke ..	70·64 mm. × 81·33 mm.		3rd gear (s/m) .. 1·357 : 1	
Cubic capacity ..	1,275 c.c.		2nd gear (s/m) .. 1·916 : 1	
Valves	Pushrod o.h.v.		1st gear .. .. 3·2 : 1	
Compression ratio 9·75 : 1			Reverse .. .. 3·2 : 1	
Carburetter(s) ..	2 SU HS2		Final drive .. 3·444 : 1	
Fuel pump ..	SU electric		M.p.h. at 1,000 r.p.m. in:—	
Oil filter ..	Full flow		Top gear .. .. 16·05	
Max. power ..	76 b.h.p. at 5,900 r.p.m.		3rd gear .. .. 11·8	
Max. torque ..	79 lb. ft. at 3,000 r.p.m.		2nd gear .. .. 8·4	
			1st gear .. .. 5·02	

The 1275 is neither as smooth nor as quiet as lower output engines in the series but runs sweetly enough between its regular idling speed and 6,000 r.p.m., the irritating gear-lever chatter that afflicted earlier Coopers having been cured by rubber damping in the remote control linkage. On the other hand, the old Mini problem of stiff and jerky throttle movement was aggravated by rapid response from the engine.

Like all SU carburettered B.M.C. engines, this one starts very easily, hot or cold, and although a touch of choke is needed after a night out in the open, it can be returned after a few hundred yards without fear of stalling or hesitant pulling.

Considering how hard this car was driven, the overall petrol consumption of 29.9 m.p.g. is not bad even by Mini standards, and extremely good in relation to other cars of similar performance. We recorded nearly 50 m.p.g. at a steady 30 m.p.h. but it would be deceitful to suggest an overall figure within 15 m.p.g. of this, restrained driving being unnatural to the car and probably to most of its owners. The 9·75 : 1 compression ratio demands expensive petrol to avoid any trace of pinking at low engine speeds on an open throttle.

The Car

IN MOST other respects, the 1275S is identical to the 1171 we tested before (April 24th, 1963). The brakes are superb, a powerful servo reducing effort without sacrificing feel or progressiveness. Large (7½ in.) front discs stop the car very quickly without fade from high speeds in a dead straight line but they became a little heavier and less true after a long spell on M1 in the wet. The engine itself provides unusually strong braking on a trailing throttle.

Dunlop SP41 tyres (C41 tread on SP braced tread carcase) are equally good. Although they howl when provoked, their adhesion is enormous and probably accounts for the unusual neutral handling when cornering on the overrun: most Minis display more oversteer under similar conditions. Even so, with the 1275's extra power, throttle steering is very pronounced, strong understeer being induced under power especially on a wet road when it can be aggravated by wheel spin.

to a muffled rumble which touched our mechanical sympathy to the extent of easing the throttle. Cruising at 90 m.p.h. (5,600 r.p.m.) seems well within the car's limits if you accept the accompanying 20 lb. drop in oil pressure to a little below 50 p.s.i. The optional oil cooler (which our test car did not have) might well be fitted as standard equipment to counter both this and the enormous oil consumption. On SAE30 oil, we were getting little more than 75 miles to the pint—a costly and inconvenient thirst which we satisfied by storing large numbers of pint cans in the door pockets and topping up every two hours or so. This excessive consumption is not an unhealthy sign since the mechanical tolerances of the engine are intentionally large to ensure sufficient lubrication under extreme conditions.

Performance

Conditions: Weather: Warm and dry, negligible wind. (Temperature 57°–59°F, Barometer 29·7 in. Hg). Surface: Dry concrete. Fuel: 101 octane (R.M.).

MAXIMUM SPEEDS

Mean lap speed banked circuit...	96·8 m.p.h.	
Best one way ¼-mile	98·9	
3rd gear	75·0	
2nd gear	52·0	
1st gear	31·0	
" Maximile " Speed: (Timed quarter mile after 1 mile accelerating from rest)		
Mean	95·3	
Best	95·8	

ACCELERATION TIMES

0-30 m.p.h.	3·6 sec.	
0-40	5·6	

0-50 ...	...	...	...	7·7
0-60 ...	...	...	...	10·9
0-70 ...	...	...	...	14·4
0-80 ...	...	...	...	20·9
0-90 ...	...	...	...	37·5
Standing quarter mile		...		18·2

m.p.h.				Top sec.	3rd sec.
10-30 ...	...	...	...	7·8	5·4
20-40 ...	...	...	...	7·6	5·1
30-50 ...	...	...	...	7·3	5·1
40-60 ...	...	...	...	7·7	5·3
50-70 ...	...	...	...	9·2	7·0
60-80 ...	...	...	...	11·5	—
70-90 ...	...	...	...	15·6	—

BRAKES

Pedal pressure, deceleration and equivalent stopping distance from 30 m.p.h.

lb.	g	ft.
25	0·47	64
50	0·96	31

FUEL CONSUMPTION

m.p.g.

Touring (consumption mid-way between 30 m.p.h. and maximum less 5% allowance for acceleration)	34·6
Overall	29·9
Total test distance m.p.g. = 9·45 litres/100 km.	
	1,560 miles

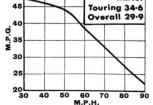

M.P.G. Touring 34·6 Overall 29·9

OWNER'S VIEW

Since the vast majority of all the surviving road-equipped 'hot' Minis are actually Mini-Coopers, rather than Cooper Ss, the author chose to talk to two enthusiastic owners of the former, one of whom kindly provided his car for photography into the bargain. These interviews give an interesting insight to Mini-Cooper ownership in the 1980s.

First of all, the author talked to David Nutland, who is not only a keen area organiser of the Mini-Cooper Club, but owns a very rare derivative (in the UK) of these cars, an Innocenti 1000.

AAGR: Tell me how you got involved in Mini-Coopers?
DN: Right from my childhood, I suppose, for my uncle had a Mini-Cooper when I was five or six years old! Then I was soon caught up with the Paddy Hopkirk, racing, rallying, thing. That was nearly 20 years ago, and I'm only 27 now!
AAGR: So when and how did you start motoring, then work up to the Innocenti?
DN: My very first car was an ex-autocross Mini, beaten up, slightly tuned, and red with a white roof, as they all have to be! From there I inherited the family Riley Elf, which I've still got, and I installed an MG1100 engine in it. I'd got the bug by then, but an Escort, then a Chevette, went with my job, then of all things I started seeing this

Innocenti in Bournemouth. After I had pestered, and pestered, the Italian owner, he eventually agreed to sell it to me, and it was still left-hand-drive of course.
AAGR: How different is it from a British-type Mini-Cooper?
DN: The rolling shell is pure Cooper S, but Innocenti offered a choice of engines – the 998cc or the 1275cc. Mine had the 998cc engine, which Innocenti always fitted with a Cooper S camshaft, and a slightly higher compression ratio. Interestingly, I know now that the bonnet, boot, roof and wing panels are all slightly different – the boot simply because of the different licence plate recess, the other panels having slightly different shapes.
AAGR: It must be very rare in the UK?
DN: I think mine is the only 1000 in the country, but I think at least 100 Innocenti 1300s are now in the Mini-Cooper Club.
AAGR: What sort of condition was it in, when you bought it?
DN: Well, let's just say that it had already gone through five Italian owners, though bodily it was pretty near perfect. Except that it must have been on its roof more than once, because we found an inch of filler there when we cut out the hole for the sunroof! It was simple to convert from left to right-hand-drive, for except for needing a new rack, almost all the other fittings just swopped over. Mechanically I had to rebuild it extensively, for it had almost 'been round the clock' before I bought it.
AAGR: Is this the only Mini you have?
DN: No, I am also completely restoring a 1071S, for use in competitions. The problem is that I can get things like rods, cranks and pistons, but there don't seem to be any cylinder blocks. You can't use a 1275S block, which is too tall, and if you skim one down, then there are water pump problems and the head won't fit. So perhaps I will have to start with a full-race, 1293cc unit.

AAGR: Do you use the Innocenti every day, or is it a 'toy'?
DN: I use it every day. I used to have a company car, but not any more, and this means that I am clocking up more than 20,000 miles a year with the Innocenti. I think it handles superbly, even though it has 'wet' Hydrolastic suspension; that's odd, by the way, for mine is a '72 model, and all UK Minis were 'dry' again by this time.
AAGR: Tell me a little about the owner's club? It's still growing fast, isn't it?
DN: Yes, though perhaps not as rapidly now, which might mean that most of the remaining Mini-Coopers have been found, and rescued. We have no links with the other Mini clubs, and although they have been very helpful at times, particularly in loaning cars for exhibitions or major club meetings, we really have very limited links with Austin-Rover.
AAGR: What about the supply of spare parts?
DN: Really there are so many suppliers now specialising in Mini bits .... but if we go into a local BL/ARG dealer and ask for factory parts, we tend to get the reply 'Not available'. If ARG have parts on the shelf for too long, they tend to scrap them, which is a great shame. A lot of rare parts are disappearing.
AAGR: Are these cars still good value today, and which type do you prefer driving?
DN: You get very much what you pay for, though it would be a costly Mini-Cooper which fetched more than £2000. A Cooper S might be a bit more expensive. Actually I think an S can be a bit of a pig to drive, while a 998 Cooper is a beautiful little car to drive around. A Cooper S can be a rough car to drive, the engine is so much rougher as well – a tuned 998 can be quicker anyway, and so much more pleasant.
AAGR: Have you ever been tempted away from the Innocenti, into hot Escorts, MGBs, or whatever?
DN: No. An Escort never appealed,

27

the only thing that did was a Twin-Cam (Lotus) Cortina, and I almost bought one before buying the Innocenti, because the price was similar. Ideally, I admit that I'd like a Golf GTI to drive on the road every day, and a Mini-Cooper specifically for competition.

Keith Redwood, whose white car (with a black roof) is pictured in this book, was equally emphatic about his love for the little Mini-Coopers.

AAGR: When and how did you get involved in Mini-Coopers, and is this the first one you have ever had?
KR: I bought this one nearly three years ago, but it's the first Mini-Cooper I've ever had, though I've had various other Minis.
 The first one was an ordinary 1969 Mini 1000, but the floor rusted and fell out of that, so I bought a 1974 Mini 1000. Eventually I stumbled on this car by chance – I was looking through the local paper, the *Echo,* one night, and saw an advert for a 'Low mileage/one owner Mini-Cooper'. I went round on the off-chance to have a look at it – and bought it!
AAGR: So, what sort of condition was it in?
KR: Structurally and mechanically it was very good. The recorded 28,000 miles from new was obviously genuine. But it was absolutely filthy, and covered in muck. It needed a real clean up, and a bit of bodywork had to be repaired. There was slight rust on the bottom of one of the doors, which is a common problem, and on the rear valance.
AAGR: It looks nice, and absolutely standard. Is it always like that?
KR: Not quite. The engine is quite standard, though normally I use a set of Cosmic alloy roadwheels. I put it back to standard trim for photography!
AAGR: Do you hope to keep it a long time?
KR: Oh yes, I hope so. I use it for business every day, and it's the only car I've got. Incidentally, you may have noticed that I have transferred

my personalised registration number to it – it had a local number when I bought it.
AAGR: Once insuring a car like a Mini-Cooper used to be difficult. How old are you, and is insurance still a problem today?
KR: I'm 25, which means that the insurance bill is not too bad now, and the fact that it's a 998cc model helps too. Last year (1983) I paid only £130, for a fully-comprehensive policy, and the notional value of the car is taken into account in the policy.
AAGR: It looks so nice – do you have to put in a lot of effort to keep it looking good?
KR: Yes, I suppose so. I clean it a couple of times every week, underneath perhaps every two weeks or so, and I clean out the inside regularly. It's serviced regularly, too, I do that myself.
AAGR: Do you have a problem getting any parts? In fact, have you needed many parts?
KR: I haven't needed much, it is a reliable car, but you can get the majority of stuff quite easily.
AAGR: The majority of bodywork is still available, isn't it?
KR: Yes, wings and stuff like that. Things becoming hard to get are items like boot lids and bonnets ...
AAGR: Are they not the same on 1980s Minis, then?
KR: ... No, slightly different. Many people actually modify modern parts to fit. Earlier Minis had double-skin boot lids, the later ones have a single skin, and later cars have different mounting brackets, while the moulding where the number plate fits is different. It's not too worrying, right now.
AAGR: Do you drive it fast, and do you enjoy it?
KR: Yes, though I don't hammer it, and I do observe speed limits. But there's no problem in keeping up

with any other traffic. The handling is tremendous, of course – mine's a 'wet' one, by the way.
AAGR: Have you modified the suspension, and did you have to have it pumped up at all?
KR: No, it's absolutely standard – the 'wet' suspension is a little less firm than the 'dry' ones, but I've got used to that. It was a little down at the rear when I bought it, but I soon had it pumped up, and it's fine now.
AAGR: I'm sure you don't need 'tame' specialists to help you keep going?
KR: No, not at all. There are several – like Cooper Car Components of Romsey – and all the Mini specialists can supply parts, but it doesn't matter much as yet. Basically it is trim and things like that which are becoming difficult, but mechanical stuff is still available.
AAGR: Does you car suffer from any of the traditional old Mini problems – like drowning in wet weather, water leaks, and so on?
KR: No, I've never had any of that sort of trouble. It starts first time every morning, and it's never ever let me down.
AAGR: Do you have any desire to get a Cooper S, to replace this car?
KR: No, I'm happy with the one I've got. But if I had the money, well maybe as an extra car to play with, then maybe I would ....
AAGR: Okay, I understand, but the Cooper S is more 'fashionable' than the Mini-Cooper isn't it?
KR: In the club yes it is, but personally I'm very happy with this car.

BUYING

I propose to make this quite a personal section, not only because I have strong views about the merits of the various model derivatives, but because the 'nuts and bolts' of Mini-Cooper purchase have now been well-covered in almost every automotive 'classic' or 'enthusiast' magazine.

It is worth pointing out, right from the start, that although a large number of cars were built in ten years (and for five more years in Italy), the supply of sound examples is rather llimited today.

Best Buys?

On the assumption that there is enough choice between the various types, I would like to review, briefly, the merits and known drawbacks with each derivative. In the context of this book, I have to consider five types:

997cc Mini-Cooper
998cc Mini-Cooper/Innocenti 1000
970cc Mini-Cooper S
1071cc Mini-Cooper S
1275cc Mini-Cooper S/Innocenti 1300

I can eliminate any tiny body differences, for in spite of the use of Austin and Morris badging, each and every UK Mini-Cooper was built at Longbridge, by the same workforce, to the same quality standards. They were all two-door saloons, and at no time were there any 'de Luxe' or 'Super' versions of the basic mechanical model.

997cc Mini-Cooper. This was effectively only on saie for two years, and about 25,000 were built. I never liked the use of the long-stroke engine, and quite a number of the endemic early Mini quality problems were still present. The later, 998cc version was a much more appealing machine.

998cc Mini-Cooper. The unsung, unpublicised, hero of the Mini-Cooper years. Announced after the Cooper S began to win all the competitions, and make all the headlines, the 998cc car was significantly quicker, had a smoother short-stroke engine, and was put together better than the original 997cc car. Recommended. Approximately 76,000 built.

970cc Mini-Cooper S. The archetypal 'homologation special', surprisingly 972 cars were built in less than a year. Shortest stroke/most peaky/highest revving of all the breed, always felt 'fussy' and undergeared. Half of the cars were 'wet', many of them exported when new. Very rare — are *any* road cars left?

1071cc Mini-Cooper S. The original, and (for road use) the sweetest of all Mini-Cooper S types. In spite of the over-square engine, surprisingly docile and lusty, ultra-reliable. Few optional extras on the production cars (unlike mid-life 1275S), and many cars later up-engined to 1275 cc specification. Only 4017 built in less than two years. Nevertheless, my favourite, if you can find one.

1275cc Mini-Cooper S. 40,449 owners couldn't be wrong, surely? This was the lustiest, torquiest, of

all, but some say the long-stroke engine was rough at high rpm, and eventually chewed up its transmission. Even so, specially balanced units were silky smooth, and even when slightly tuned the performance was phenomenal. Get a 1966-1968 model, perhaps, to enjoy most standard equipment (twin tanks, oil cooler, etc), but be sure it has 'never been raced or rallied'. Most were!

In summary, my two favourite types are the 998cc and 1071cc models, though I know the 1071cc is now rare on the road. Buy one to cherish — you should not be disappointed.

Is everything what it seems?

I won't go into detail, but it is really very easy to 'create' one type of Mini from another. If you are looking over a car preparatory to purchase, be absolutely sure that it *is* what is advertised. A close study of chassis, engine and body numbers will help, along with knowledge of suspension and body style features.

But is it really a Cooper S 1275cc engine/transmission, or has it been transplanted from an MG 1300, or similar — there is a significant difference? How do you know that the 998cc engine is genuine Mini-Cooper, or converted Mini 1000 — for there are ways of telling the difference? Do the brakes match the rest of the specification? If originality matters to you, is the car you inspect 'dry' when it should be 'wet', or is it really a MkII or a MkI with some MkII features. Are you sure that it is a Morris as badged, or partly Austin under the skin? Many, many Mini-Coopers have been 'created' as rebuilds of rally cars, or conversions of less exciting models, so I really must stress this caution.

What are the desirable 'extras'?

Fortunately, this little section shouldn't become very confusing for, as I have said, there was only one trim specification for each model, and only one body style.

Although there was almost a limitless list of extra equipment which could be fitted to the cars to make them faster, and more competitive (either supplied by BMC/BL's Special Tuning division, or by private specialists), there was really not much which was ever fitted on the production lines at Longbridge.

From 1966, of course, the 1275cc Mini-Cooper was fitted with twin fuel tanks, an engine oil cooler, wide-rim wheels, and solid inner driveshaft U/Js (and reclining seats were already optional), many earlier cars had some of these items fitted, and there were even some Mini-Coopers (not Ss) which had some of these options installed as well.

It is also traditionally desirable to have a two-tone Mini-Cooper (in which the roof panel only is a different paint colour from the rest of the body) — though, of course, it is easy enough for you to modify a Mini-Cooper that way after you have purchased a monotone machine.

Other buying hints

On the question of 'wet' and 'dry' suspension, I recommend that you try out both types of car before you decide. 'Wet' suspension was not adopted until the start-up of 1965 model year production, and gradually phased out before the end of the 1960s. This was not just because it was less satisfactory than 'dry' suspension in the main, but because it cost considerably more.

'Wet' suspension has often been accused of promoting a noticeably see-sawy front-to-rear ride (and certainly, by comparison with 'dry' suspension it is not as firm), but you must certainly try a car thoroughly before disregarding it out of hand. Don't forget, for instance, that in every other way, the 1966-1969 Cooper S was the best equipped of all Mini-Coopers.

Don't be put off by a car that is visibly non-standard. It would be nice to think, of course, that all the standard bits are still available, but there is nothing wrong with a Mini-Cooper which has a leather or wood-rimmed steering wheel, a different driving seat, light-alloy road wheels, and other extras, for many such accessories were used when they were current models. I would be far more worried about a car that was obviously highly tuned, and had straight-cut gears, ultra-hard suspension, and the slots and holes remaining after the removal of extra lamps, sump guards ...

Do be sure that the car of your choice still runs straight. Once a Mini-Cooper has been crashed, or even after an arduous competition season, it never seems to run straight again, probably due to the distortion of the front or rear subframes. It might feel all right from inside the car, but it might be crabbing visibly, and tending to wear its tyres prematurely. Is the handling predictable, left to right? Follow the car down the road, and see if it sits square and true?

Corrosion. There isn't space to go into all the obvious corrosion potential of a Mini-Cooper. Let me just say that there is lot of it about, but that you can keep a very doggy bodyshell! running for years just so long as the subframes are in good condition. Knowledgeable Mini-owning friends will know where to look — take their advice.

Front end problems. Once again, no space to go into detail, but the two obvious 'what to look for' points include the condition of the driveshafts (especially on high-power Ss) — if they have started clicking on lock, expense lies ahead — and whether there is a tendency of the car to overheat. The overheating might just be due to a radiator whose vanes are blocked (this can be cleaned by a judiciously applied water hose), but it might indicate something more serious.

Lastly, don't be rushed into buying the first superficially glossy car you find. (Strangely enough, Keith Redwood, whose 'Owner's View' precedes this section, did just that, but he has been lucky). There are enough Mini-Coopers around, if you have patience, for you to make the right marriage. A good buy can be a joy for years to come.

CLUBS, SPECIALISTS & BOOKS

Clubs

Although nearly five million Minis of all types have been built, including well over 100,000 Mini-Coopers of all types, there are very few specialist clubs catering for enthusiast owners. In the UK, the most important is undoubtedly:

The Mini-Cooper Club,
9 Walesbeech,
Furnace Green,
Crawley,
West Sussex,
England. (Tel: 0293-542812)

— which concentrates on sport and fellowship, along with the collection and provision of technical advice on restoration, and the sourcing of hard-to-find spares. The club is also building up a list of known, and approved, specialists in Mini-Cooper work, so any new Mini-Cooper owner should hasten to join.

The Mini Owners Club,
18 Mercia Close,
Coton Green,
Tamworth,
Staffs,
England. (Tel: 0827-52858)

— covers all Minis, not merely Mini-Coopers, and provides the same type of service as the Mini-Cooper club.

If you are a racing person, there is also:
The Mini-Seven Racing Club,
141 Walton Drive,
Terriers,
High Wycombe,
Bucks,
England. (Tel: 0494-26414)

Specialists

More than a decade after the last British Mini-Cooper was built, BL Cars are still producing more than a thousand ordinary Minis every week, which means that many parts common to the Mini-Coopers are still in large scale production.

For that reason, and the fact that BL parts stocks are still in reasonably good shape, there has not been much call for true 'preservation' specialists to emerge.

Mini-Cooper enthusiasts told me that although there are literally dozens of tuning firms who can provide competition parts, and preparation expertise, the following are the best-known concerns for restoration, and specialist production supplies.

Cooper Carponents,
The Old Works,
Crook Hill,
Braishfield,
Romsey,
Hants,
England. (Tel: 0794-68344)

— providing original parts, and original optional parts, especially for Cooper and Cooper S models.

Mini Spares,
21/31 Friern Barnet Road,
Southgate,
London N11 1NE,
England. (Tel: 01-368-6292)

— mainly providing mechanical parts, and some body spares.

Mini Sport,
Thompson Street,
Padiham,
Lancs,
England. (Tel: 0282-78311)

— not only provide many competition parts, but a big choice of standard engine and gearbox components.

Avonbar Racing Ltd.,
219 New Haw Road,
Addlestone,
Weybridge,
Surrey,
England. (Tel: 0932-42024)

— well-known for concentrating on Mini-Cooper competition parts.

Books

It took time for books about Minis, and Mini-Coopers, to begin to appear, but the choice is now wider than ever before. The subject is covered in many ways, from the factual to the philosophical, from touring to motorsport. I think the most significant titles (apart from this one!) are:

Mini-Cooper and S, by Jeremy Walton. This is one of the Auto History series, by a well-known Mini lover, a compact little title which covers the background behind the cars, and the author's own experiences of them. Published by Osprey.

Mini, by Rob Golding. To celebrate the Mini's 20th birthday, Rob Golding, then the *Birmingham Post's* motoring correspondent, wrote a complete history of the Mini project, complete with prototype pictures and production figures not previously seen. A big, ambitious, book published by Osprey.

The Works Minis, by Peter Browning. Browning was employed at Abingdon when the

Mini-Cooper competition saga began, and became Competitions Manager in 1967 after Stuart Turner moved on. Extremely detailed, and naturally authentic story of the 'works' competition cars' careers. Published by Haynes/Foulis.

Mini-Cooper, 1961-1971. Is a Brooklands Book product, entirely comprised of reprints of magazine tests and impressions of the cars when they were in current production. For that reason, lacks historical perspective, and hindsight, and all the 'warts' stay well hidden. Published by Brooklands Books.

How to Modify Your Mini, by David Vizard. Is an amazingly detailed book about the tuning of chassis and engine of all types of Mini, with competition in mind. Invaluable to the Mini-Cooper owner, especially one whose car might have become non-standard before he bought the car. Excellent for 'picking' ideal camshaft profiles, carburettor details, and cylinder head casting details, for instance. Published by Fountain Press.

Tuning BL's A-Series Engine by David Vizard. Simply the most up-to-date and comprehensive manual on tuning the A-series engine available. Published by Haynes/Foulis in Autumn 1984.

In case you do not have a Workshop Manual, and cannot find the official BL example, consider: **Mini (1959-1969) Workshop Manual, by Haynes.** This is prepared by expert Haynes staff specially in the overhaul of all types of car, and has many step by step explanations of how to keep in health, or restore to health, the various Minis including all members of the Mini-Cooper family. Published by Haynes.

Lastly, there is one gem of a book, long out of print, originally published with BMC's help, in 1964:

The Mini Story, by Laurence Pomeroy. Pomeroy, once an esteemed technical editor of *The Motor,* was a technical consultant to BMC in later years, and collaborated closely with BMC's Alec Issigonis and other BMC executives to produce *the* inside story of the birth and development of the design. Quite easy to find at autojumbles and in specialised motoring book shops, and well worth the search.

PHOTO
GALLERY

1

2

1. Mini-Cooper origins! This was the first-ever BMC
Mini mock-up of 1957, coded 'XC9003'. Much was to
change in the next couple of years, but the basic
proportions were never changed. The material, by the
way, is wood!

2. This is an original 948cc A46-engined AD015
prototype, where the carburettor faced forward. It first
ran before the end of 1957, and reputedly had near-
Mini-Cooper performance, but was then de-tuned for
production as BMC management thought it 'too fast'

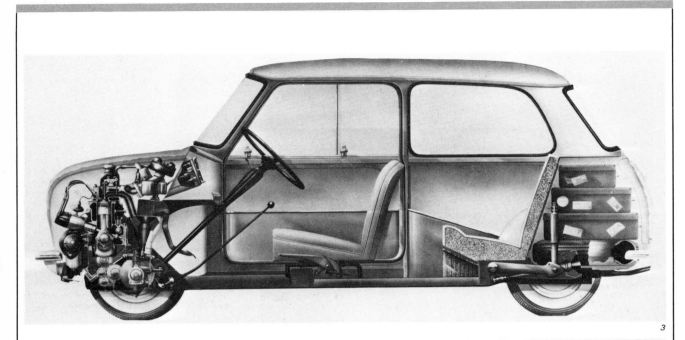

3

4

3. The Mini, as put on sale in August 1959, was a mere 10 feet long, with an extremely compact engine bay. In this form, of course, it had an 848cc engine, and a long willowy gear-lever.

4. In 1965 the Mini's engine/transmission/subframe power pack looked like this, with a single semi-downdraught SU carburettor, and with Hydrolastic suspension. Compare it with ...

5

6

5. ... the similar-in-concept Mini-Cooper power pack, in this case with 'dry' suspension, but complete with twin semi-downdraught carbs, tubular exhaust manifold, tiny disc brakes, and remote control gearchange.

6 & 7. Two views of a Mini-Cooper S engine, in something like 'show' condition, though without the remote control gearchange fitted. The 16-blade fan created a noticeable whine. The ignition leads on this example are non-standard. Note the way the spark plugs and distributor were ideally placed to pick up spray through the grille on early examples. This unit has an inertia starter and a dynamo, but pre-engaged starters and alternators are often found on restored or rebuilt Mini-Coopers. It doesn't matter if the rocker cover says 'Austin' or 'Morris', for all were built on the same assembly line at Longbridge!

8. The man who thought of the Mini-Cooper in the first place was John Cooper, one of the pragmatic geniuses behind the Cooper GP Car programme of the 1950s and 1960s.

7

8

9

10

9. The four most important personalities in the saga of the Mini-Coopers, posed in front of Paddy Hopkirk's 1964 Monte-winning 1071cc Mini-Cooper S. Right to left, they are: Alec Issigonis, Charles Griffin, John Cooper, and Bill Appleby (in glasses). Standing rather diffidently in the background, behind John Cooper's right shoulder, is Daniel Richmond (of Downton Engineering) whose tuning expertise became legendary among Mini owners.

10. A series of noses. Here is an original 1961 pre-production 997cc Austin Seven Cooper (to use the correct title), on test by the press at Chobham ...

11. ... but this version is slightly more 'standard' because its wheels are covered by hub caps. The bonnet badge states 'Austin Cooper' ...

11

12

13

14

12. ... which, when the car in question became a Mini-Cooper S, had a chrome letter 'S' fitted above it. This, to be precise, is a pre-launch 1071S of 1963, supplied to the press with 4.5 inch rim wheels, but no hub caps and no wheel arch extensions!

13. The Austin Cooper was shown at the Paris Salon in 1961 in this guise, left-hand-drive of course, but with whitewall tyres. The bumper corner guards between overriders and ends were standard.

14. More noses ... this being a 1961 launch picture of the Morris Mini-Cooper, complete with 997cc 55bhp engine, and bumper corner guards. The bonnet badge, of course, was different from the Austin, as was the grille ...

15

16

17

15. ... but when the Mini-Cooper S derivative came along, it was only necessary to add the 'S' letter above the bonnet badge. The tyres on this 1963 model are Dunlop SP3s, with a very coarse tread.

16. A close look at the nose of this 997cc Morris Cooper shows the words 'Morris' and 'Cooper' on each side of the fording ox in the bonnet badge — even though the car was always built in the Austin factory at Longbridge!

17. On the first 997cc Mini-Coopers, the tyres had a puny 5.20 section, and were Dunlop C41 crossplies. Do you remember Gold Seals? Note, too, the familiar external body panel flanges, and the sliding windows in the doors.

18. When the Mini-Cooper became MkII in the autumn of 1967, it was given an all-synchromesh gearbox (not all Minis had them until mid-1968), a slightly larger rear window, a modified bonnet badge, and a larger front grille. The paradox, here, is that the car is badged as an Austin (and, in fact, is a 1275S) but has what we would previously have called a 'Morris' grille. The grilles were standardised by this point ...

19

18

20

19. ... as this study of a 1969-model Austin Mini-Cooper 1000 confirms. The grille is the same, as are the SP41 tyres, but the wheel trims are different, as is the bonnet badge.

20. The first Mini-Cooper S MkII of 1967/1968, showing off its larger tail lamps, the standardised 'Mini-Cooper S MkII' bootlid badge, and the twin fuel filler caps denoting an 11 Imperial gallon fuel capacity. It

may be difficult to spot the difference, but the MkII rear window was a bit larger than before. 1275 tells its own story, surely!

21

22

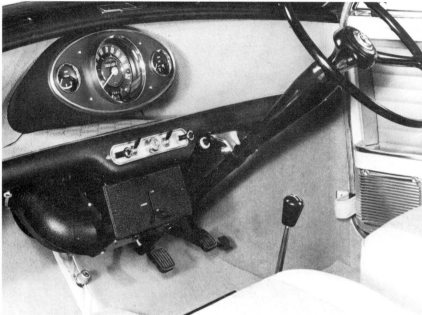

23

24

25

21. Identification test? In fact this is an early Morris Cooper S engine bay, showing the twin carburettors with their simple flame-trap air cleaners. The engine bay, complete with fresh air heater, is full – but on the competition cars it could be even more crowded!

22. The 1969-model MkII Cooper S, complete with 1275cc engine, had a 'proper' air cleaner for its SU carburettors. This particular car has oversized (1½in.) carbs.

23. Detail of the instruments and controls of the Mini-Cooper S, original (ie MkI) variety, showing the very simple heating/ventilation controls, the floor-mounted dipswitch, and the hand-operated press-stud for the windscreen washer (close to the steering column bracket). The speedometer read up to 125mph, which was optimistic, to say the least!

24. The Mini-Cooper of 1965 had an 'office' typical of its type, with the four-instrument central display (Four? Yes – the fuel gauge is in the base of the speedometer), the remote control gearchange, the sliding door windows, and the rather casually fitted floor carpets. The radio on this particular car was not standard. What, no safety belts?

25. Compared with the MkI, this pre-release picture of the MkII Mini-Cooper S instruments and driving position shows few changes, except the deletion of the floor dipswitch – and the increase of speedometer calibration to 130mph!

26

27

28

26. A different one, this! Actually an Innocenti Mini-Cooper 1300, a car built in Italy until the mid-1970s, with a choice of 998cc Mini-Cooper or 1275cc Mini-Cooper S engines. The Rostyle wheels were standard in later years on these cars, while the winding windows with fixed quarter windows were exclusive to the Innocenti derivative.

27. The facia display of the Italian Innocenti 1300, much smarter and more informative than that of the home-market Mini-Cooper S. I wonder why it was never even considered by British management?

28. This is how an Innocenti 1300 (Cooper S engine) announced itself on the bootlid.

29

30

31

32

33

29. A 1974 model of the successful Innocenti 1300, really a 1275S in all but name, but with extra equipment.

30. MkII UK-built Cooper S cars all shared this bootlid badge, without reference to marque. The MkII was introduced in the autumn of 1967.

31. Before 1968, your Morris Cooper (MkI) had a badge like this, but only the Mini-Cooper S (970, 1071, or 1275cc) had the simple 'S' above it on the curve of the bonnet.

32. ... whereas this was the MkII's front badge, with 'Austin' or 'Morris' as appropriate.

33. One interesting way to modify a Mini-Cooper S, was to give it a hatchback. This was Minister of Transport Ernest Marples' own car in the 1960s.

34

35

36

37

34. The cast alloy (magnesium on the competition cars, aluminium on others) Minilite wheel was a popular fitment to Mini-Coopers.

35. The car British Leyland hoped would replace the Mini-Cooper in the enthusiasts' hearts – the 1275GT, complete with long-nose, Rostyle wheels, and single-carburettor engine. It sold quite well, but the character simply wasn't there any more.

36. In the early 1980s, John Cooper looked all set to produce a new 'Cooper', this time the MG Metro Cooper – but BL's hierarchy would not back it, and refused copyright permission to use the name on such a car. For a time Cooper thought of selling it as the 'Monaco', but the project folded when BL refused to honour warranties for the rest of the structure.

37. If the MG Metro of the 1980s is the Mini-Cooper reborn, then this machine, the MG Metro Turbo, is a latter-day Mini-Cooper S, but without the zing or the precise handling.

38

39

40

41

38. The 'Holy of Holies' – the 'works' competitions department at Abingdon, when the Mini-Cooper S ruled the roost in European rallying. No. 242 was actually Rauno Aaltonen's Group 1 1275S, under preparation for the 1966 Monte Carlo Rally, where it finished second to Makinen's sister car, but was then disqualified in the famous 'headlamps fiasco'.

39. 569 FMO was a 'works' rally car, a 1071S, built up for the 1964 Monte Carlo Rally, and this was its engine compartment, complete with oversize carbs and intake trumpets. There isn't much space for anything else in that engine bay!

40. The first truly famous Mini-Cooper S rally victory was at Monte Carlo in 1964, when Paddy Hopkirk was the driver. 33 EJB is now retained in the BL Heritage historic collection.

41. Another famous Mini-Cooper S victory was by Paddy Hopkirk in the 1967 Alpine Rally, which was one of the fastest road events ever promoted. This 1275S had a long and honourable career, and was always used in highly tuned form. According to the grille it is an Austin, but there isn't a bonnet badge to prove this! The '6' near the competition number indicates the Appendix J Group.

42. AJB 33B was originally a 1275S 'works' rally car for the Acropolis rally of 1964, but on the 1965 Alpine rally (seen here), Timo Makinen and Paul Easter drove it into second place in the Touring Car category.

43. Ah! Here is a 'works' rally car, not only with a proper grille, but a matching bonnet badge as well! LBL 666D, in fact, was being driven on the 1967 Monte Carlo rally by Paddy Hopkirk, and finished sixth. Naturally it was painted red, with a white roof!

44. Not just any old Mini-Cooper racing shot, but one showing a privately-owned Morris, being overtaken by Warwick Banks' 'Cooper Car Co' Austin, and by John Handley's 'Broadspeed' Morris, at Oulton Park, in 1965.

45. When John Rhodes' 'Cooper Car Co.' Morris Cooper S was drifting neatly, it was tidy and always had the legs on fast Anglias like Anita Taylor's, which is behind it. On the other hand ...

46. ... when Rhodes was not only scrubbing off speed, but cornering very sharply indeed, the tyre smokescreens could be truly spectacular.

49

50

47

48

NPL 830D

51

4900 KR

52

53

47. A contrast in tail lamps. This is the original MkI type, used until autumn 1967 ...

48. ... when the larger MkII lamp was phased in.

49. On the MkI Mini-Coopers badged as 'Austins', the name was spelt out in neat script on the boot lid. This contrasts with ...

50. ... the Morris Cooper MkII identification on a 1969 model.

51. When we photographed two nicely preserved cars especially for this book, it was interesting to compare the original 1966-type MkI nose with ...

52. ... the MkII nose, where the grille was enlarged, and where the same grille was used for Austins and Morris types.

53. Even though this little car was built down to a budget, BMC found time to produce a nicely detailed 'Austin Cooper' bonnet badge for MkI models ...

54. ... but the MkII bonnet badge was not nearly as distinctive.

54

55. Front corner detail of a 1966 Austin Mini-Cooper, with the characteristic bumper corner guards, the amber-lensed direction indicators, and (on this car) the optional 4.5 inch rim wheels.

56. All the best Mini-Coopers were duo-tone, with the second colour only applied to the roof panel. Except on liveried competition cars, any form of striping was not quite the thing!

57. When you have looked at this nicely-preserved, 18-year-old example of a 998cc Mini-Cooper, you wonder why they could not all have been made with wide-rim wheels and duo-tone paintwork!

58. The original stop/tail/direction indicator lamp was the same as that used in all other Minis, by Joseph Lucas, and was quite vulnerable to damage.

59. On MkII bootlids, the engine size (1000 or 1275) was noted by this neat little badge on the lower corner.

55

56

57

58

59

60

61

62

60. Open up the bootlid of a Mini-Cooper and you find a small luggage locker. On late-1960s Cooper S cars it was even smaller, due to the fitment of two fuel tanks, one each side. The battery lived under the plywood platform supplied to support luggage.

61. Nothing complex about the door 'furniture' of a MkI or a MkII Mini-Cooper or Cooper S, for both types had sliding windows, and those useful stowage bins, ideal for slotting in maps (for rallying), or — they say — milk bottles or wine!

62. The simple sliding window locks of Minis of the 1960s. Unfortunately, these cars are quite easy to burgle, so be warned.

63. The door release handle, inside the Mini-Cooper door. It could be even more crude than this, for on early non-Cooper models, there was a pull string instead!

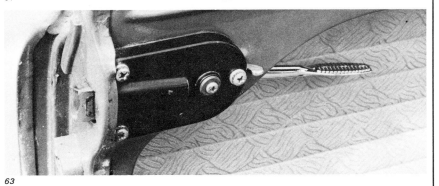

63

64

65

64. The small luggage boot of the Mini-Cooper, showing the plywood floor, which covers the spare wheel position and the battery (which is towards the offside). The second fuel tank, when fitted, occupies the empty space on the right side. As on all such Minis (this is a 1969 MkII) the number plate swings down when the lid is lowered.

65. Not many people seem to use the rear seats of Mini-Coopers, but if they did, they would find adequate space. There is a lot of stowage space under the cushions, by the way.

66. This is so typical a stance for a Mini-Cooper — square, purposeful, compact, and obviously ready for anything.

67. Most Mini-Coopers ended up being personalised in some way — Keith Redwood's sports his own personal number plate, wing mirrors and modern radial ply tyres.

66

67

C1

C2

C1. *Real car, but false snow! This is the genuine 1965 Monte Carlo Rally winning 1275S, AJB 44B, on display some years later. The same car, extensively rebuilt, won the 1982 Lombard-RAC Golden 50 rally as well.*

C2. *Another rare bird, though there is no badging to prove it – this is one of the short-stroke 970cc Mini-Cooper S cars, built only in 1964 and 1965. According to the registration plate, this is one of the last ones to be sold.*

C3

C4

C5

C3 & C4. A delightful 1966 998cc Austin Cooper, MkI pictured in 1984. You can read about this car in the 'Owner's View' section.

C5. This is a 998cc Mini-Cooper MkII. If it was a 1275S, the only difference from this angle would be in badging, twin fuel tank fillers, and a larger-bore exhaust pipe.

C6

C7

C6. There isn't a wasted inch anywhere in the packaging of a Mini-Cooper. This is a 1969 model, in MkII guise.

C7. When a shape is right, it looks good from any angle. From the sheen on that roof panel, it looks to be clean enough to eat your breakfast off!

C8

C9

C8 & C9. The Mk II 998cc Mini-Cooper, as sold all over the world. The only noticeable improvement for the MkIII Cooper S was to fit wind-up door windows. A lot of potential motoring enjoyment – for racing, rallying, autocross, or just for open-road fun in a package just 10ft long. In the 1960s, and even today, what could be better?

C10

C11

C10. White with a black roof, a sunroof and Minilite wheels as accessories, so very typical of a 1275S of the 1969/70 MkII variety.

C11. The very last MkIII Mini-Cooper S cars had wind-up door windows, and yet another type of boot lid badge; twin fuel tanks were retained. The wheel arch extensions on this car, though of the officially homologated type, were not standard.

C12

C13

C14

C12. Rare in the UK – The Italian Job, being a 1974 Innocenti 1300, converted to right-hand-drive.

C13. The Innocenti 1300, complete with 1275 S engine and transmission, had an instrument binnacle of entirely different design to the UK version.

C14. All UK-built Mini-Coopers had this simple instrument display, with the speedometer also housing the fuel gauge, flanked by oil pressure and water temperature gauges. On this particular car, the left-hand gauge is non-standard.

C15

C16

C17

C15. The MkI 1275S engine bay, nicely preserved on this enthusiast's car (the picture was taken in the 1980s), though the alternator is a later and worthwhile modification.

C16. On the first series of Mini-Cooper S Models, the Morris versions had boot lid identification like this ...

C17. ... while the Austins looked like this, which means that different piercings were needed in the boot pressing!

C18. Rear identification of the Morris Cooper, MkII version, as always with a simple T-handle to open the boot.

C19. The still-born MG Metro Cooper project outside John Cooper's own garage premises on England's south coast. Even a name change, to 'Monaco', could not persuade BL to back it with a warranty, or approval. What a pity ...

C18

C19